Faith-Based Caregiving
in a
Secular World

Faith-Based Caregiving in a Secular World

Four Defining Issues

James J. Londis

James J. Londis
Faith-Based Caregiving in a Secular World: Four Defining
Issues/James J. Londis

ISBN 978-1-60743-317-0

Printed in the United States of America

DEDICATION

This book is dedicated to caregivers past, present and future. In my own past, the faithful caregivers within the Kettering Health Network in Dayton, Ohio earned my admiration each day they followed the example of Jesus as they served their patients. Also in the past are the devoted caregivers in my own family who eased the death of the people they most loved; my mother-in-law Arlene who cared for my father-in-law Charlie, and my brother George who cared for my sister-in-law Regina.

In the present, hundreds of thousands of Christian caregivers in faith-based as well as secular healthcare systems and companies minister curing and healing each day to people in suffering. They deserve our highest honors.

Lastly, the caregivers of the future: my students at the Kettering College of Medical Arts and all those who will, in time, care for sick or disabled children, siblings, spouses, and parents—may God bless you in your selfless service.

CONTENTS

ACKNOWLEDGEMENTS

I wish to thank Bonnie Casey for her superb editorial assistance in the development of this book. She made it better in so many ways and encouraged me throughout its writing.

My thanks also to Fred and Aura Lee, Robert Smith, Daryll Ward, Cleta Nelson, Ted Hamilton, my son Jeff, my daughter-in-law Yolanda, my daughter Lori, my wife Dolores and others too numerous to mention who read early versions of the manuscript and offered constructive suggestions to improve it.

Gratitude also extends to my son-in-law William Dwyer for designing the cover and the format of this volume.

I am blessed to have these wonderful people in my life.

Introduction

Before the astounding medical breakthroughs of the last century, healthcare measures were largely high touch, aimed at healing broken spirits and relationships in the absence of effective cures for disease. When a cure did take place, it was often a happy accident. As I once heard a Harvard Medical School professor say, "the history of medicine is the history of the placebo effect." Today we are seeing an explosion of medical technology, from diagnostic imaging to promising treatments for cancer and HIV infection. Oddly, however, these improvements in the realm of cure have been accompanied by a decline in what I call healing. Patients' social, emotional, and spiritual needs have largely melted into the background. Wounds are treated, but not woundedness.

At first, as this imbalance became more pronounced, church-affiliated hospitals fought a mostly losing battle to maintain a spiritual ministry to their patients. The economics of modern healthcare pushed the funding of spiritual care, which was seen as having little or no impact on health, way below the bottom line. Science-based cure was all that mattered, a consequence no doubt of the Enlightenment's emphasis on the rational. But the loss of focus on healing left a serious deficit. Of course patients wanted their physicians and nurses to be up on the latest science in order to provide a cure, but they also wanted their spiritual needs to be acknowledged. As practically the only providers of spiritual care in the hospital setting, chaplains began to feel marginalized, while nurses, physicians, and technicians did the "real" work of healthcare. Today however, thanks to patient dissatisfaction with the lack of a spiritual dimension in healthcare, the imbalance between curing and healing is starting to be redressed.[1]

Christian spirituality—the ability to understand another's woundedness and feel as God feels about someone else—is essential to the healthcare ministry of the Christian church. This link between healthcare and spirituality has a long history. The modern concept of a hospital dates from the time of Emperor Constantine, who converted to Christianity in the 4th century CE and decreed that caring for the sick was a religious obligation. In most respects, the first hospitals were actually hospices which cared for the dying. In a hospital, at the interface of the healthcare industry and human suffering, the insufficiency of private spirituality becomes clear, because caring for the sick and dying truly does take a "village." It takes the efforts of healthcare professionals working as a team with family and friends of the patient, aided by the prayers of those who love and support them, including fellow church members. It takes a caregiver willing to engage in a spiritual ministry of healing by learning to feel as God feels about the patient.

Whether they are religious or not, most sick or dying patients long for an experience of God. Doctors, nurses, and chaplains often hear such sentiments as, "I want to feel God close to me as I go through this," or more poignantly, "I want to know God loves me and is not punishing me." They welcome prayer at their bedsides and treasure spiritual conversations with anyone who will take the time. And they benefit from these encounters in unexpected ways. Studies show that spiritual interactions improve medical outcomes. Patients who share a prayer with their surgeon or surgical staff are better able to tolerate anesthesia and remain more stable throughout the procedure. Hospice patients acquire a special peace through prayer as they sense God's presence and are convinced of their future with God. In my experience as a pastor visiting members in the hospital, I have seen that when a patient expresses peace and a sense of God's presence, their loved ones too feel their own anxieties diminish.

Developing empathy for the woundedness of the sick confers a powerful gift of healing, as my son experienced several years ago when his father-in-law suffered a massive stroke. A prominent and respected psychiatrist, cherished as the patriarch of his family, he was now dependent on a wheelchair. During a family visit, my son helped this once proud man out of his wheelchair and onto his bed for a rest. "Dad," said my son, "it must be awfully hard to have a body that won't do what you want it to do."

"You have no idea," he replied, "how I hate being such a burden."

This man, who for decades had willingly shouldered the burdens of his wife, children, patients, and coworkers now grieved over this deep wound to his self-esteem. For a once virile man who loved to ride horses and play golf, being confined to a wheelchair was a spiritual and emotional calamity for him and his family. How could he *not* feel diminished? And yet, I am certain, sharing that burden with his son-in-law, and having his pain understood and accepted, was a gift of healing to his broken spirit.

The sickest and weakest among us are most in need of a new vision of themselves and their value. Drug addicts, the homeless, sick children, the aged—their great need diminishes their ability to see themselves as Jesus sees them. And while physicians, nurses, and other caregivers must do everything possible to address their physical infirmities, a Christian healthcare ministry must also help patients see themselves as God sees them. Like all who are broken by life's unfairness and tragedy, if they are open to God's presence, God will comfort them in the special way they require. According to the Bible, God feels our woundedness—our sickness, brokenness, loneliness, and isolation from each other—and suffers with us.

Our passion for God's presence and consolation for our spiritual woundedness intensifies when we are sick or dying. When we are healthy, it is easier to deceive ourselves into believing we are invulnerable, that we do not need God's grace and healing. But when sickness or disability strikes, we cry out for God's presence. Broken bodies, which remind us of our mortality, drive us to seek God's consolation more urgently than ever before.

In the reflections that follow on the role of Christian spirituality in healing and healthcare, forged during my years as a pastor, professor, and hospital ethics resource, I offer the reader my own way of understanding these universal issues. It is my prayerful hope that this small book will enlighten, stimulate and comfort those who read it.

James J. Londis
2009

Notes and References

[1]As an example, see Elaine J. Yuen's editorial "Spirituality, Religion, and Health." *American Journal of Medical Quality* (Vol. 22, No.2, Mar/April 2007), pp. 77-79.

Issue One

∽

Healing Beyond a Cure

Cure May Not be Enough

I heard an unforgettable presentation not long ago at a conference on church-related hospitals. A missionary physician serving the Seminole Indians in Florida told a story about a boy who came to the clinic because he'd fallen off his bicycle and broken his ankle. The doctor set the ankle, put it in a cast, and sent the boy home, confident that he had done all that was needed for the boy to recover.

A few days later, Buffalo Jim, the tribe's medicine man and healer, encountered the doctor and asked about the boy. The doctor said, "I set the bone and the boy will recover just fine, Jim. No need for you to worry about him." But the medicine man, who did not seem convinced, replied gravely, "Setting the bone will not be enough to heal the broken ankle."

"What are you talking about?" the doctor asked, doing a quick mental inventory, trying to recall some test or procedure he might have overlooked in caring for the boy.

But Buffalo Jim wasn't interested in the doctor's skill at taking x-rays and setting bones. Instead he asked, "Do you know *why* the boy broke his ankle?"

"Of course," replied the doctor, confident he was back on solid ground. "He fell off his bicycle."

"That is *how* he broke his ankle, but not *why*," replied the medicine man. After a pause he said, "The boy broke his ankle because he had a fight with his mother, jumped on his bicycle, and rode away so furiously that he fell." Buffalo Jim looked the doctor in the eye and said without hesitation, "The ankle will not be healed until the boy and his mother are reconciled."

Buffalo Jim's prescription for healing may sound odd to a culture like ours, steeped in medical knowledge and with a near worship of science. After all, a broken bone is one thing; a spat between a mother and son is another thing altogether. Modern physicians are trained to set bones but not necessarily to repair a son's relationship with his mother. But Buffalo Jim never disputed the value of modern medicine. Of course setting the broken bone was the appropriate therapy, and he didn't question the doctor's ability to perform that task with skill. But the medicine man knew that a broken ankle was only part of the boy's problem—he also suffered from a broken relationship. Therefore, in the Seminoles' view, fixing the boy's broken bone was a necessary cure, but an insufficient *healing*.

Buffalo Jim's views on the limitations of modern medicine reveal a stark contrast between a scientific culture's beliefs concerning the causes and cures of disease and those of a nonscientific culture. Western medicine looks for the cause of disease, such as physical trauma, bacteria, or genetics, and prescribes a biological or physiological cure. But the Seminoles, and other like-minded cultures, see diseases, broken bones and wounds in a larger context where, for the purposes of our discussion, they become "illnesses." Removing shrapnel from a wounded soldier does not remove his battle-related nightmares. Providing medicines for a pneumonia patient may cure her disease, but her fear that it may leave her with permanent deficits is an illness that requires healing.

My 93-year-old father lives in a retirement community in Florida with his 88-year-old wife of more than 30 years. Some time ago he called and urged me and my wife Dolores to come down to see them. I knew that my stepmother had been growing weaker and had started using a walker, but I sensed that something else was wrong—my father had never summoned me like this before. Dolores and I prepared to leave for Florida, having arranged for my two brothers to meet us there a day later. But just as we were leaving, a nurse from my father's retirement community left a message on my cell phone that my father had had an "episode" that required a visit by EMTs and an overnight stay in the hospital for observation. Even more alarming, she told me my father had recently been hospitalized for four days with a bleeding ulcer that had required minor surgery. This experience had left him weak and exhausted, resulting in the current crisis.

When we arrived at the apartment, we were shocked at my father's appearance—he was clearly distraught and even had a splotch of blood on his arm. He explained that his wife had fallen the night before and, in struggling to assist her, he had scratched himself. Things gradually calmed down and the next day, after my brothers arrived, we decided to take my father to his country club to play some golf. My middle brother and I hit some balls on the driving range while Dad and my younger brother watched from a golf cart.

We decided to have lunch in the club before taking Dad home, but before our food was brought to the table he looked at me and said, "I feel woozy. I need to go home right now." Without discussion, I drove him back to his apartment, where he went directly to bed and took a long nap. We were all growing confused and alarmed by now, but later that evening Dad said he was feeling fine. Nevertheless, Dolores and I accepted his invitation to come with him to his next doctor appointment.

A day or two later, we were driving Dad to his appointment when he started talking about his doctor and the special arrangement he had with him. Dad was paying his physician an additional fee each year for "concierge" service. This gave him and my stepmother access to the doctor at any time, for any need, with no waiting. The fee even entitled them to house calls if needed. "He's saved my life three times, Jim,"

Dad told me solemnly, and I could sense his deep respect and appreciation for the doctor I was about to meet.

As soon as we entered the office, we were pleasantly surprised by the warm ambience. Coffee, fruit, and muffins were available in the well-appointed suite. The receptionist even offered to make our coffee and fill a plate for each of us if we wished. After a brief wait, the doctor appeared and invited us into his office. What followed was truly astonishing and gratifying.

To assure himself that Dad's faculties were intact, the doctor began quizzing my father on his medications; type, dosage, frequency. He dug a little further and discovered that Dad had not been taking his prescribed sleeping pills nightly, but only when he thought he needed one. Things began to make sense to us then. Dad would go to bed without taking his medication and sleep for three or four hours, only to wake up and not be able to go back to sleep. So he would take a sleeping pill in the early morning hours, which explained his wooziness and fatigue during the day. The doctor quickly deduced that my Dad's anxious desire to be alert and watchful during the night in case his wife needed his help was keeping him from taking the necessary steps to recover from his hospitalization, compounding his distress and exhaustion.

The doctor gently but firmly counseled my Dad, showing him research indicating that it takes many weeks for a man his age to recover from the loss of strength imposed by a long hospitalization. "You must take a sleeping pill each night before you go to bed—no exceptions. You will be of no use to your wife if you do otherwise," he advised. For another hour, this wise, warm-hearted physician explored the difficulties my father and stepmother were coping with. He assured Dad that he would come to see my stepmother if she could not come to the office. It was clear to me that the doctor had a close relationship with my father, that he cared a great deal about him as a person and not simply as a patient.

As we were leaving the office, Dad mentioned that I had worked in healthcare for quite some time. The doctor accompanied us to the waiting area and told me that, while he objected to the connotations of the term "concierge" medicine and realized that this service was not financially feasible for everyone, it nevertheless allowed him a medical practice that was fulfilling and joyous. Because his practice is limited to a fixed number of patients, he can spend as much time as necessary with each one. He had spent well over an hour with my Dad addressing his medical, emotional, and social needs. This special arrangement gave the doctor the time and luxury to "heal" his patients' illness, not just "cure" their sickness.

§

The Biblical View of Illness

As I reflected on the stories of Buffalo Jim and the encounter with my father's physician, I realized that Buffalo Jim's belief in an unassailable link between physical health and spiritual well-being and the Florida doctor's fulfilling medical practice each pointed the way both forward and backward: back to a pre-scientific world view and forward to a necessary course correction for modern-day caregivers.

In the world described by the Bible, physical and spiritual wholeness were understood in a way that, at some level, might have resonated with Buffalo Jim. To understand that world, we must imagine a culture with no knowledge of the causes of disease, and without even the basic understanding of biology, genetics, and chemistry that we expect of every modern American high school student. Without scientific explanations for the plight of the sick and disabled, especially those afflicted from birth, the people of Jesus' time were forced to fall back on religious explanations, a fact that had an enormous impact on social relations and community behavior. John Pilch, a medical anthropologist trained in New Testament studies, has written of this period, "The sick affected the entire village, hence they were of concern to the entire village."[1] Because people's primary concern was maintaining community holiness and human relations, anything that upset social integrity had to be rooted out, usually through separation and isolation, before it could infect the whole community. Because social relations and kinship were the dominant realities of people's lives in that period (Pilch, pp. 67-68), no greater punishment could be inflicted than being cut off from the community. Disease and disability were seen as evidence of an offense against God, while at the same time sinfulness and moral failings were judged as a kind of illness. So the New Testament describes both the sick and the sinful—the blind, crippled, and insane as well as prostitutes and tax collectors—as rejected by God and under divine punishment. They deserved to be outcasts from the circle of kinship and community. No matter what their particular affliction, or how simple and straightforward their diagnosis would be today (glaucoma, scoliosis, schizophrenia, to name just a few), the sick in ancient Palestine were marginalized, ostracized, and, worst of all, treated as "unclean." Being "cured" of the sickness was understood to mean God was no longer angry with you. If you now belonged to God, you could once again fully belong to the village and synagogue.

In Jesus' time, the condition characterized by red, flaky skin, known then as leprosy but now believed to be some form of psoriasis, marked one as out of the ordinary. People who contracted "leprosy" were declared unclean, shunned, and forced to remove themselves from the community (Lev. 13:45-46). For a member of a collectivistic society, such excommunication was devastating—the equivalent of a death sentence (Pilch, p. 41). Wherever they are used in the Bible, the words *leprosy* and *leper* carry this horrible stigma. On more than one occasion, a leper came to Jesus and begged, "Lord, make me *clean!*" (see Luke 5:12-16), a request not so much directed at the skin condition as at the experience of being rejected because one is "polluted."

But according to the New Testament, it was not just lepers who were left to fend for themselves. Many who were crippled and blind had to beg to survive. The lame man who lay on a mat beside the pool of Bethesda (John 5:12-14), waiting for an angel to "stir the waters" to manifest the pool's healing power, had "no one to help him" get into the pool. Having no one to help him suggests a profound isolation for someone from a culture focused on kinship and relationships. Why else would the poor man's family, friends, and neighbors refuse to help him if not for the fact that his condition had made him "untouchable"?

The Gospel of Luke recounts another occasion when Jesus encountered one of society's outcasts, a blind man isolated by his community, with no one to comfort him in his misery and need:

> As [Jesus] approached Jericho, a blind man was sitting by the roadside begging. When he heard a crowd going by, he asked what was happening. They told him, "Jesus of Nazareth is passing by." Then he shouted, "Jesus, Son of David, have mercy on me!" Those who were in front sternly ordered him to be quiet; but he shouted even more loudly, "Son of David, have mercy on me!" Jesus stood still, and ordered the man to be brought to him; and when he came near, he asked him, "What do you want me to do for you?" He said, "Lord, let me see again." Jesus said to him, "Receive your sight; your faith has saved you." Immediately, he regained his sight and followed him, glorifying God; and all the people, when they saw it, praised God (Luke 18:35-43).

If his blindness is gone, he must be in God's favor and we can accept him back into the community. In other words, he is *healed*.

§

Illness in Modern Times

It would be difficult to overstate the radical differences between the world we know now and the world of the early Christian era. For one thing, we live in a culture deeply committed to individual freedom, not social responsibilities. Our family and community relations are neither the all-encompassing reality of our lives nor the primary basis for understanding ourselves and world events. We live in a cocoon of social isolation imposed not by expulsion from the community, but self-imposed by cars, computers, and an obsessive focus on privacy. Furthermore, centuries of intellectual inquiry and scientific investigation have brought about a radically different understanding of the causes and cures of disease.

And yet, there seems to be a persistent and tragic holdover from ancient times. To a disturbing degree, we still tend to isolate the very sick, the severely disabled, and the old and dying, albeit for different reasons. We may not "drive them from the village," so to speak, but we accomplish the same thing by placing them in a variety of healthcare facilities where they are too often cut off from the healing support of community.

But why is this so, given the fact that we no longer think of the sick as "unclean"? Studies reveal that, perhaps for different reasons, both family members and healthcare providers have a tendency to distance themselves from the gravely ill and dying. In a youth-oriented, career-driven, status-obsessed culture, people grappling with disability and disease remind us of what we work so diligently to ignore: our own fragility and mortality.

I was in a shopping mall recently when I noticed a young woman making her way around the shops in a wheelchair. It's a common enough sight these days, but it nonetheless gave me pause. The woman looked as though she had cerebral palsy, a condition shared by a good friend of mine in Maryland. I am quite comfortable accompanying this friend in public places, yet the woman in the shopping mall disquieted me. "What is this about?" I wondered. Why are we undisturbed by the sight of someone with their leg in a plaster cast, and yet find even television images of amputees returning from Iraq upsetting? Is it because the former can be cured while the latter cannot? Are those of us who are able-bodied bound to be unnerved by chronic, untreatable conditions? Such reflexive responses can make interacting with the sick and disabled difficult even for the most caring individuals. We self-consciously ask ourselves, "If I try to connect with them will they assume my efforts are born out of pity and resent me for it? If I avoid looking at them, will they feel ignored and marginalized?"

This tendency to personally isolate the sick and disabled is played out on a communal level as well. Perhaps we don't overtly ostracize these people whose presence we find so disturbing. We don't need to. We just make sure that most of them don't enter our field of vision. For generations, public buildings were constructed as if everyone could climb stairs, and the few builders who did install elevators didn't take into account how the blind might use them. Even after elevators became commonplace in very tall buildings, like the Empire State Building in New York, it took an act of Congress to require new construction of more than one floor to have elevators large enough to accommodate a wheelchair and to have Braille floor indicators. Still today we have countless subtle and not-so-subtle ways of ostracizing the mentally impaired, AIDS patients, smokers, the obese, the very short, the very tall, and the very eccentric. What we fail to realize is that their isolation often causes more suffering than their physical or personal challenges.

§

Modern Medical Practices

Regrettably, as highly trained and skilled as they are, modern-day healthcare providers are simply not equipped to provide a level of care that would offer healing—a return to wholeness—as well as a cure for disease. Such an approach goes beyond science. In ancient cultures, any attention given to the sick and dying was, to use caregiver jargon, strictly "high touch." How could it have been otherwise, since there was no high tech to draw on? But as a result of modern medical advances, especially those of the past 75 years, healthcare in Western cultures has become almost exclusively high tech and has lost nearly all of the high touch dimensions of patient care. Imaging machines that help us see inside the body have replaced the time we used to spend looking into the mind and feelings of the sick. This circumstance is exacerbated by our current system of healthcare reimbursement, for as you might guess, high tech is more expensive, and thus more lucrative, than high touch. To put it bluntly, cutting pays better than listening.

This situation has not arisen because doctors and nurses are inherently heartless, or because healthcare workers are more greedy and grasping than the rest of us. It is the result, for the most part, of an underlying "triage ethic" motivating most medical practices today, that is based on a calculus employed in catastrophic emergencies. The principle of triage emerges from a strictly rational approach to bioethics that, of necessity, must think of a patient strictly in terms of disease and cure, taking little or no account of the needs of the patient as a whole or his relation to a larger community. When a calamity such as a fire, earthquake, or airplane crash severely taxes existing medical resources, triage requires caregivers to sort the injured into three groups: (1) those who are dying and cannot be helped by medical intervention, (2) those who are critically injured but can be rescued with intervention, and (3) those who are injured but not in immediate danger of dying. In such a circumstance the hopeless receive comfort care if it is available; otherwise, they are left to die. The injured receive minimum care, while critically injured but treatable victims are given immediate, intensive care. Triage is all about disease and cure.

Another factor influencing modern medical practice is simply that human resources are stretched, sometimes to the breaking point. Modern healthcare is expensive. Overtaxed by duties that include monitoring patient meds, IV's, and vital signs, buried under a mountain of paperwork, some nurses tell me they deeply miss the dimension of personal care that attracted them to the profession in the first place. Oncology nurses, in particular, have one of the highest burnout rates in the medical professions. I have shadowed nurses and physicians in their daily routines and been astonished that between the vagaries of "staffing to the grid" in nursing and the demands of tightly scheduled physician office visits, these professionals have little if any time for more than perfunctory personal interaction with their patients. "Treat 'em and street 'em" is how one physician characterized medicine today. A nurse I shadowed on the medical unit literally ran from room to room, and even then had difficulty administering meds to her patients on time. How could she possibly provide high touch care as well? How could she hope to minister to her patients' spiritual and emotional needs?

Thankfully, our culture no longer assumes that the sick and disabled are sinful and thereby rejected by God. In fact, in a promising trend, the medical profession is recognizing its responsibility to humanely manage pain for dying patients, and to keep them comfortable while offering them a dignified death. Still, many have noted a tendency for healthcare workers to gradually abandon terminally ill patients. Because of the pressures noted above, there is a subconscious but perceptible diminishing of contact with such patients. Because of their training and limited resources, physicians and nurses tend to devote more energy to those they may still be able to help. In addition, they will admit, some of the testing they do is defensive medicine to protect them against legal action. They must focus on curing, which means the healing has to be done by others: chaplains, family members, close friends. Families must go into the hospital to provide a timely glass of water, a plump pillow, or a back rub. In this regard, the growing practice of hospice care is a welcome throwback to a time when people died at home, surrounded by people who loved them, comforted by familiar, homey things such as family pictures or a favorite quilt.

§

Illness and the Social Network

Fortunately, there are hopeful signs that our culture is seeking a new direction that acknowledges both the differences and the profound connection between conditions that need curing and those that require healing. Doctors, social workers, and ministers alike are recognizing the link between broken relationships and physical abuse, between emotional distress and physical breakdown. Unfortunately, this realization came too late to help my mother, who suffered for decades with physical problems that resulted from feelings of abandonment and loneliness. She was the child of her mother's second husband who, it turned out, already had a wife in another state. My grandmother and he separated, leaving my mother without a father's daily presence in her life. When he passed away a few years later, my mother's feelings of loss were incalculable. She knew that, whether or not anyone else in the family loved her, her father had loved her deeply, and for that she loved him more than anyone else in the world. She never recovered from losing him.

Looking back, I believe that this loss partly explains why my mother became pregnant with me at the age of seventeen. By the time her marriage to my father collapsed seven or eight years later, she had two more sons and was forced—as a single mother—to raise the three of us on welfare. For comfort, my mother ate and chain-smoked. Physicians who, though well-meaning, nonetheless addressed cure rather than healing, gave my mother diet pills to help her lose weight, merely adding addiction to her catalog of personal problems. When my stepfather phoned me one night and began by telling me that I should sit down, I was sure he was calling to tell me that my 83-year-old grandmother had passed away. When I heard instead that it was my 52-year-old mother, I could hardly believe it. The cause of her death was officially listed as stroke or heart attack, but I knew better.

My mother's case is a microcosm of a worldwide problem: the illnesses that come from broken human relationships, broken communities, and broken societies. In our own time, the AIDS epidemic has taught us that organic disease cannot be disengaged from "diseased" social networks. The missionary physician who told the story of Buffalo Jim ended his presentation by asking, "What do you think is the single greatest cause of disease in the world today?" My mind raced through a list of deadly bacteria and viruses, but the speaker's next sentence caught me off guard. "The answer is poverty," he said, "not viruses, not mosquitoes, not bacteria—*poverty*. Nothing would improve world health more dramatically or more completely than eliminating poverty." When I had time to reflect, I realized the truth of what he had said. Poverty is indeed a result of the breakdown of economic structures and social networks. Lack of clean water, sufficient nourishment, and adequate shelter breeds disease, while economic security and strong communities foster health and well-being.

The kind of "illness" caused by poverty and social breakdown is often experienced as grief and oppression. In extreme instances, loss of attachment to human society leads to loss of meaning. Philip Yancey, an award-winning evangelical author, writes, "An alcoholic in Australia told me that when he is walking along the street he hears the footsteps of everyone coming toward him or passing him becoming faster. Loneliness and the feeling of being unwanted is the most terrible poverty."[2] Yancey quotes Mother Theresa, the Albanian nun who devoted herself to the homeless in India, as saying, "We have drugs for people with diseases like leprosy. But these drugs do not treat the main problem, the disease of being unwanted. That's what my sisters hope to provide" (Yancey, p. 173). She also believed that the sick and poor suffer more from rejection than from material want.

While we don't usually think of grief as an illness, it too is an oppression brought on by a severed relationship. The loss of a spouse or child can create a veritable vacuum in one's life. A few weeks after the death of his wife, my brother George said to me that he was struggling to find a new meaning for his life. "It's hard," he said. His wife's death was the end, in many ways, of his social network. He didn't have a disease, but he did need to be healed. Physicians tell me that anxiety, depression and addiction are more prevalent in their patients than are hypertension and diabetes.

§

Jesus' Ministry to the Sick

In Jesus' day, as we have seen, misfortune of any kind, including disease, was interpreted as an offense not only against social values and norms, but against God as well. Jesus' treatment of the sick and disabled who sought him for help was in many respects a frontal assault on this cultural attitude rooted in that religious belief. Notice the following New Testament episode:

> As [Jesus] walked along, he saw a man blind from birth. His disciples asked him, "Rabbi, who sinned, this man or his parents, that he was born blind?" Jesus answered, "Neither this man nor his parents sinned; he was born blind so that God's works might be revealed in him" (John 9:1-3).

As Pilch comments, unlike most of those around him, Jesus is more concerned with the symptoms than with the cause of a disease. He sees the man's blindness as "not the cause but rather the manifestation of the misfortune, the symptom." Jesus' cures are thus "symptomatic rather than aetiological therapies" (Pilch, p. 13). In other words, Jesus countered the conventional view that a person's misfortune was the result of offending God by dealing with the symptoms without passing judgment on the origin of the suffering. At the same time, Jesus knew that, given the attitudes of his contemporaries, one who was sick could not be restored to total wellness unless the people around him were convinced that the perceived offense to God had been removed. For people who believed that the cause of a person's misfortune was God's displeasure, rejecting and isolating the sinner were logical responses. For them, blindness was merely a sign of a larger problem—God's displeasure—not the problem itself. Jesus knew that to be healed, the sick must be restored to God's favor in the eyes of the people, even as their physical problems were cured. For as long as the ill were seen as incurring God's disfavor, they would continue to experience excruciating rejection from the community. In other words, without experiencing God's forgiveness and having that forgiveness understood by the community, curing the sickness would be almost useless.

After Jesus had invited Levi to become his disciple, we read in Luke:

> Then Levi gave a great banquet for him in his house; and there was a large crowd of tax collectors and others sitting at the table with them. The Pharisees and their scribes were complaining to his disciples, saying, "Why do you eat and drink with tax collectors and sinners?" Jesus answered, "Those who are well have no need of a physician, but those who are sick; I have not come to call the righteous but sinners to repentance" (Luke 5:29-32).

Being cast out of the community because they were sinners imposed a serious illness of its own, not unlike that which afflicted the blind and the lame. Christ's mercy and compassion *heal* because through him, sinners are accepted back into the community and cleansed of their "pollution." Pilch writes, "In the context of health and well-being, the things that ailed people derived principally from socially rooted symptoms involving the person in society, rather than from organic and impersonal causes" (Pilch, p. 122). That is why, while all symptoms are important to Jesus, "the social ones receive special attention" (Pilch, p. 122). Some people, especially those with a high regard for modern science, question whether the miracles credited to Jesus in the New Testament actually represent cures of specific diseases and disabilities. Whether or not you believe that physical cures did in fact happen during Jesus' ministry (as I do), *a cure is different from a healing.*

Luke also tells the story (vs. 8:42b-48) of a woman who had suffered from hemorrhages for twelve years. No one had been able to cure her, Luke says, setting the stage for her dramatic encounter with Jesus. In a crowd, acting alone, not wanting to be identified for all the reasons we have mentioned, the woman touches the "fringe" of Jesus' garment, a piece of blue cord that hung from the garments of observant Jews to remind them of certain Scriptures. As Luke recounts, her hemorrhage stopped immediately. Jesus reacted by asking who had touched him, which seemed like a silly question to his disciples since they were being jostled by a huge crowd. When no one came forward, Jesus persisted, "Some one touched me; for I noticed that power has gone out from me" (vs. 46). Realizing she could not remain hidden, the woman, trembling from the impact of her experience, fell at Jesus' feet and declared that she was the one who had touched him, and that she had been *immediately* healed. Jesus comforted her by telling her to go in peace; "your faith has made you well" (v. 48).

Anyone with such a condition would naturally want to remain hidden since exposure might result in social isolation. Margaret Mohrmann, a physician and professor of Christian ethics, says that Jesus insisted on knowing the woman's identity because he would not allow any "faceless" healing in his ministry.[3] I suspect that Jesus insisted that the woman identify herself so that, in Richard J. Beckman's words, she "could know the joy of being restored to full acceptance by her neighbors."[4]

§

Restoring Wholeness through Healing

While the "illnesses" of isolation and loneliness cannot be *cured*, those who experience them can be healed. When my brother George's wife Regina was dying from a brain tumor, to my surprise, and with my admiration, George made the decision to care for Regina at home rather than have her spend her final days in a hospital or nursing home. George admitted that he made the decision knowing nothing about what was involved in caring for someone who was terminally ill, but he was retired and figured he had the time to learn. Over time, George learned how to administer Regina's meds for her intensifying headaches. But he also discovered that he was not alone in his high-touch endeavor. Regina's sister and brother-in-law came weekly to visit her and offer some relief to George, and even the neighbors pitched in with generous offerings of support. Soon, caring for Regina had truly become a community project. When I visited Regina during this time, it was clear that being in her own home, surrounded and cared for by people she knew and loved, was the best comfort and support she could have had on that most painful, lonely, and frightening journey.

While the principle of triage mentioned earlier makes rational and ethical sense, on an emotional and spiritual level it does not leave caregivers feeling that they have done the *right* thing, only that which is *less wrong*. Only someone who perceives healing as a calling from God can ignore triage ethics. Mother Theresa, as we have seen, was an embodiment of how the reign of God summons us to relate to illness differently than the world now does. Mother Theresa challenged the practice of abandoning Calcutta's dying poor in the name of triage by opening a clinic just for them. She insisted that God had called her to care for them first. Her goal was that each of these outcasts would die in a clean bed, with something sweet to eat (which in India only the wealthy can afford), and the comfort of a human presence. Such an approach could not be justified on strictly rational grounds, but she defended it by stating that she was not a social or healthcare worker, but a *religious* one.

Mother Theresa recognized the truth that healing goes beyond curing bodily disease. It includes the thoughts, feelings, and behavior of the whole person in his social and cultural context. We cannot cure all types of cancer, but we can try to heal a cancer patient's hopelessness and depression. We can fit an amputee with a prosthetic limb, but we must also strive to restore his joy of living. "Illness is the loss of meaning in one's life. Healing restores meaning, all the time, infallibly," says Pilch (p. 130). This is the religious and spiritual task of modern healthcare.

Rachel Naomi Remen is a pioneer in the field of mind-body holistic health and one of the first physicians to recognize the role of the spirit in health and recovery from illness. In her book *Kitchen Table Wisdom*, Remen tells the story of a patient who looked for healing from the physician he trusted to cure him:

> For some time now Dieter had suspected that the chemotherapy was no longer helping him. Convinced at last of this, he spoke to his doctor and suggested that the treatments be stopped. He asked if he could come every week just to talk. His doctor responded abruptly. "If you refuse chemotherapy, there is nothing more I can do for you," he said.
>
> Dieter had felt closed out and pushed away. "When I talk about not doing more chemotherapy, my doctor becomes all business. We are usually friends, but when I mention this his friendship cuts off. He is the one I talk to. His friendship means a lot to me." And so Dieter had continued to take the weekly injection in order to have those few moments of connection and understanding with his doctor.
>
> The group of people with cancer listened intently. There was another silence, then Dieter said softly, "My doctor's love is as important to me as his chemotherapy, but he does not know."

Dieter's statement meant a great deal to me. I had
not known, either. For a long time, I had carried
the belief that as a physician my love didn't matter
and the only thing of value I had to offer was my
knowledge and skill. My training had argued me
out of my truth. Medicine is as close to love as it is
to science, and its relationships matter even at the
edge of life.[5]

Remen then reveals that Dieter's oncologist was one of
her patients. Chronically depressed, he had come to believe
that no one cared about him, that he was just "another white
coat in the hospital, a mortgage payment to his wife, a tuition
check to his son. No one would take notice if he vanished . .
." (Remen, p. 65).

What a dilemma. When Dieter's physician could no longer offer a cure, Dieter wanted him to become a healer. Had
the physician grasped it, this opportunity to take on the role
of a healer might have contributed to his own healing. You
see, curing is always a one-way transaction from caregiver
to patient, but healing is a gift given by two people who need
healing from, and offer healing to, each other. The physician
did not see, Remen concludes, that his sense of failure in not
being able to cure Dieter's cancer kept him from receiving the
healing he himself needed.

§

Healing for Family Members

Another thing that healthcare workers today may overlook is that a patient is not a single entity, but a member of a family, and that when someone is ill, in many ways their family and friends are too. Alcoholics Anonymous, an organization with a long history of helping alcoholics deal with their addiction, recognized this fact early on and established a sister organization, Al-Anon, for spouses and relatives of alcoholics. In our efforts to provide the very best care for the sick and disabled, we mustn't forget that family members may also need their own kind of healing.

Not long ago, I visited the ICU at the hospital where I was employed as an ethics resource. A very accomplished professor of music was on life support there, and the staff told me that her husband was being surly and uncooperative. The patient's physicians and nurses had tried to explain to her husband that nothing more could be done for his wife. She was brain dead, they told him, which in clinical terms meant that her life was over in the most relevant sense. They suggested that he allow them to withdraw his wife's life support.

"Over my dead body," he had shouted, letting fly a barrage of expletives and threats of lawsuits if the hospital staff did not continue doing everything possible to keep his wife alive—or at least breathing. Understandably, the woman's caregivers ran for cover and called for reinforcements. They asked me to talk with the man to see if something could be done to alleviate his wife's prolonged suffering and minimize his own trauma. In talking to him, several things became clear to me. First, his Jewish faith and traditions were a major factor in his determination to keep his wife alive as long as possible. This could not be dismissed lightly. Second, it was obvious that he loved his wife and was deeply depressed over what was happening to her. And finally, while she was the one occupying a bed in the ICU, he too was ill and needed healing. The clinical staff agreed not to force the issue of removing life support, but to wait and see what happened. In less than two weeks, even life support was insufficient to keep the patient going. She died, and her husband said goodbye trusting that everything possible had been done for her.

Two months went by and I forgot about the grieving husband until I spotted him at the hospital one day eating lunch with a physician who was a trainee in our chaplaincy program. As soon as I had the chance, I asked the chaplain about the conversation I had witnessed. He told me that he and the man had been meeting for lunch almost weekly since his wife died. "It seems to help him," the chaplain told me, and I believe that this gesture of compassion will indeed help the man heal and again know the joy of living. This experience affirmed my belief that offering healing to the survivors and family members of the sick and dying is an integral part of Christ's healing ministry in the world.

This was again brought home to me by Fred Lee, internationally renowned speaker on healthcare and author of *If Disney Ran Your Hospital: 9-1/2 Things You Would Do Differ-*

ently, who told me about a meeting he had with a group of department managers at a major metropolitan hospital. One of the managers told the audience that his wife had had a long struggle with cancer and had died in the hospital. In anguish at the moment of his wife's death, the man had cried out to a nurse, "Where is God at a time like this?" Without hesitation the nurse had replied, "I believe God is exactly where he was when his son died; in grief, like you are now." These wise and caring words had such a powerful effect on the shattered husband that, some time later, he returned to the hospital just to express his gratitude to the nurse and to tell her how her compassion had helped him through his grief.

§

Healing When There Is No Cure

Mother Theresa knew that even the terminally ill can be healed of their feelings of hopelessness and isolation. Closer to home, we find an example of this truth in the life and words of Morrie Schwartz, the subject of Mitch Albom's remarkable bestseller, *Tuesdays with Morrie.* An immensely popular professor of social psychology at Brandeis University, Morrie, as he was affectionately known by his friends and students, was diagnosed with Lou Gehrig's disease (amyotrophic lateral sclerosis) long before his life should have ended. Knowing that he was dying seemed to give Morrie a lot to say about the meaning of life, which Albom chronicles in conversations with his former professor on a wide range of issues, including the nature of true happiness. What the book reveals, in Morrie's own indomitable voice, is not a sick man unable to be cured by science, but a dying man in the process of healing.

"Let's begin with this idea," said Morrie. "Everyone knows they're going to die, but nobody believes it. . . . If we did, we would do things differently." Morrie believed that to live well you have to stop kidding yourself about death. That you have to ". . . know you're going to die and be prepared for it at any time. That's better. That way you can actually be *more* involved in your life while you're living." He preferred the Buddhist approach to life and death. A Buddhist asks himself each day, "Is this the day? Am I being the person I want to be?"[6] Morrie believed that once you learn how to die, you learn how to live. Facing death helps you focus on the essentials. The stuff that doesn't matter is stripped away and you see everything differently.

Every Thanksgiving, the church I pastored for many years on the outskirts of Washington, DC would hold a special service focusing on praise and the giving of thanks. One year, the pastoral staff decided to celebrate the season by interviewing several church members on their experiences of gratitude. The pastor whose ministry was primarily to church members struggling with illness suggested that we interview a member who was terminally ill and facing the end of his life. With trepidation, the staff agreed.

When the interview took place, more than 2,000 worshippers were seated, while several thousand more listened on the radio. As the pastor gently led him through the interview, the gravely ill man echoed Morrie Schwartz's words to Mitch Albom: "Now, I see everything differently," he said. He told us that he listened to birds singing in the morning, something he never took time to notice before he got sick. Now, he said, sunrise and sunset thrilled him in a new way, as did the presence and affection of his family and friends. Like Morrie, even though this man's disease was irreversible, he was being healed of a larger illness.

Joseph Bernardin, the Roman Catholic Archbishop of Chicago who was later elevated to Cardinal, described a similar experience. In the months preceding his death, he wrote *The Gift of Peace*,[7] recounting his grief and sadness the moment he realized that chemotherapy was not going to arrest his cancer. A deeply spiritual man, Cardinal Bernardin began to relate his own suffering to the suffering of Christ, in the sense that any Christian facing death can experience the deep spiritual blessings of the One who endured the cross and despised the shame for the sake of His children. Fearful and depressed, Cardinal Bernardin plumbed what he believed were the spiritual depths of his journey towards death, and testified that God gave him the gift of peace. For the remainder of his life, he ministered to other victims of cancer. This was his healing.

I believe that many people can learn to "live" with their physical maladies; none of us can live with loneliness, humiliation and shamefulness. Stephen Hawking and other severely disabled people have shown us that they can live rich lives if appreciated for who they are and what they can do.

§

Healing from God

Another member of the church I pastored years ago was suffering with incurable pancreatic cancer. She herself was the wife of a pastor and a long-time member of the church, but still she was facing death fearful about her relationship to God. Raised with a strict, legalistic view of religion, she was convinced that God was punishing her for not following the rigid admonitions her elders had inculcated in her as a child. What she wanted more than anything was assurance that God loved her, that she enjoyed God's grace and the forgiveness within that love, regardless of what she believed about her own unworthiness. Once she understood the gospel as an experience and not simply as an abstract doctrine, she told me that she had been healed in the most meaningful possible way. In an anointing service in her home, she made it clear that while a cure would be wonderful, God had given her peace and joy, and that was more than enough. Her husband added: "God always answers the sincere prayer for healing, even if someone is not cured." They sensed long before I did that healing transcends curing, especially in the Christian faith.

Cardinal Bernardin learned that to be healed is to have peace in the face of suffering and death. Morrie Schwartz learned that to be healed is to find meaning in life even as one approaches death. Others find healing when their broken relationships are mended, even as their chronic disease progresses. Being accepted and embraced by the "village," by those you most love and who most love you, is the ultimate healing. A physician friend of mine believes that three things need to be said to a dying person: "I love you, I forgive you (if needed) and goodbye—I will miss you." But I would not want you to think that the God of the Bible is satisfied only with healing here and now. Jesus' rare miracles of resurrecting the dead, as well as his own resurrection, point to God's intention to provide a cosmic and final healing to the inhabitants of the world and to the whole universe. According to the Bible, wherever there is brokenness, conflict, violence, ugliness, and chaos, God's healing will eventually triumph. Notice the following passage, which makes the most astonishing claims for the life and ministry of Jesus:

> He has rescued us from the power of darkness and transferred us into the kingdom of his beloved Son, in whom we have redemption, the forgiveness of sins.
> He is the image of the invisible God, the firstborn of all creation; for in him all things in heaven and on earth were created, things visible and invisible, whether thrones or dominions or rulers or powers—all things have been created through him and for him. He himself is before all things, and in him all things hold together. He is the head of the body, the church; he is the beginning, the firstborn from the dead, so that he might come to have first place in everything. For in him all the fullness of God was pleased to dwell, and through

him God was pleased to reconcile himself to all things, whether on earth or in heaven, by making peace through the blood of his cross (Colossians 1:13-20).

According to the Apostle Paul, death is the last great enemy:

Listen, I will tell you a mystery! We will not all die, but we will all be changed, in a moment, in the twinkling of an eye, at the last trumpet. For the trumpet will sound, and the dead will be raised imperishable, and we will be changed. For this perishable body must put on imperishability, and this mortal body must put on immortality. When this perishable body puts on imperishability, and this mortal body puts on immortality, then the saying that is written will be fulfilled; "Death has been swallowed up in victory." "Where, O death, is your victory? Where, O death is your sting?" (I Corinthians 15:51-55).

According to Scripture, death is not only the end-product of disease or catastrophe, it is also the ultimate illness, for it destroys community by separating us from each other. Awareness of the inevitability of death is like an illness itself. We know it is unavoidable, yet do everything possible to ignore its approach. But it rises up anyway to remind us over and over again. Each year that passes brings us closer to its finality. As we page through the family albums and see ourselves aging, we are astonished that we have gone from being a child to raising a child to holding a grandchild in so short a time.

While I believe deeply that we can experience healing in the face of death—the kind of healing that Cardinal Bernardin and Morrie Schwartz enjoyed—God's grace would not be worth much if it let us find peace in this life, only to be locked for eternity in the grip of death. Like everyone, while I grieve over my own impending death, I also grieve for the ones I have lost: my mother, my grandparents, my father-in-law and sister-in-law, my aunt and uncle and friends. Moved by the compassion of Christ, we also grieve for God's children who suffer and die by war, violence, and oppression. For the dying, death is a release from suffering; for the living, death is the cause of suffering, the thief who steals those we love, the enemy who kills, often without warning. But the gospel message is not one of retreat or defeat in the face of death, but one of hope and victory.

This is why a Christian funeral should not be a ritual of resignation, but of defiance. As the apostle Paul puts it, "We do not grieve as those who have no hope" (I Cor. 15). In her poem "Dirge Without Music," Edna St. Vincent Millay gives voice to those who resist resignation in the face of death:

> I am not resigned to the shutting away of loving hearts in the hard ground. So it is, and so it will be, for so it has been, time out of mind: Into the darkness they go, the wise and the lovely. Crowned

with lilies and with laurel they go; but I am not
resigned.

Lovers and thinkers, into the earth with you.
Be one with the dull, the indiscriminate dust.
A fragment of what you felt, of what you knew,
A formula, a phrase remains, —but the best is lost.

The answers quick & keen, the honest look, the
laughter, the love,
They are gone. They have gone to feed the roses.
Elegant and curled
Is the blossom. Fragrant is the blossom. I know.
But I do not approve.
More precious was the light in your eyes than all
the roses in the world.
Down, down, down into the darkness of the grave
Gently they go, the beautiful, the tender, the kind;
Quietly they go, the intelligent, the witty, the brave.
I know. But I do not approve. And I am not
resigned.

As fantastic as it may sound to modern ears, the New Testament message of hope points toward the second coming of
Christ and the promised resurrection of the saints. Its defiance of death would be arrogant if not for the testimony of
eyewitnesses to Jesus of Nazareth. For Cardinal Bernardin,
hope resided in the belief that at his death he would be immediately transported into the presence of God. For others,
hope is more eschatological, looking to the end of history, to

Christ's return and the bodily resurrection of his people. One view has the Christian hope of ultimate salvation coming to each person, individually, at his or her death; the other has it coming to the entire community of saints throughout all history at the moment of Christ's return. In the former, the final healing from earthly illness comes at death. In the latter, the final healing of ourselves and the entire cosmos comes at the end of history.

In the Christian story, all creation will someday be healed of its illnesses. Not only will there be no sickness, but there will be no more death, no more war, no more crying of any kind, for the "former things are passed away. Behold," God says, "I make all things new" (Rev. 21:4). That is why the Greek word for salvation (*sodzo*) is also the word for healing. *Shalom*, which in Hebrew means wholeness and health as well as peace, is the goal of both salvation and healing. To be saved from guilt and shame through God's forgiving grace is no different than being healed. That we can be rescued from death and given hope for the future is the good news of the gospel and a message of ultimate healing. No matter what happens to us *now*, the future is assured. Whatever has troubled or limited us, whatever has caused us pain and suffering, will be finished. Such is the hope that rescues us from despair. We will be healed, *and* we will be saved.

Notes and References

[1]Pilch, John J. *Healing in the New Testament: Insights from Medical and Mediterranean Anthropology* (Minneapolis: Augsburg Fortress, 2000), 67-68. Note: With respect to John J. Pilch and other New Testament scholars, a caution might be in order. In her ground breaking book *The Misunderstood Jew,* Amy Jill-Levine insists that not all Jews during the time of Jesus represented views and behavior he challenged. Much of Jesus' teaching and action was thoroughly Jewish. In the case of the sick being "polluted" and "outcast," there are examples in the New Testament—such as the paralyzed man whose friends lowered him through the roof of the house in order that Jesus might heal him—which indicate that not all Jews ostracized the sick.

[2]Yancey, Philip. *The Jesus I Never Knew* (Grand Rapids, MI: Zondervan, 1995), 173.

[3]Mohrmann, Margaret E. *Medicine as Ministry: Reflections on Suffering, Ethics and Hope* (Cleveland: Pilgrim Press, 1995), 28-29.

[4]Beckman, RJ. *Praying for Wholeness and Healing* (Minneapolis: Augsburg Press, 1995), 9.

[5]Remen, Rachel Naomi. *Kitchen Table Wisdom: Stories That Heal* (New York: Riverhead Books, 1996), 64-65.

[6]Albom, Mitch. *Tuesdays with Morrie* (New York: Doubleday, 1997), 81.

[7]Bernardin, Joseph Cardinal. *The Gift of Peace* (New York: Double-day, 1997).

Issue Two

∽

Christian Spirituality and Healthcare Ministry

In his book *Strong at the Broken Places*, best-selling author Richard Cohen, who suffers from multiple sclerosis, profiles the lives of five people struggling with chronic illnesses. One of them, a young woman named Denise who has amyotrophic lateral sclerosis (known as ALS or Lou Gehrig's disease), finds that most people she encounters are thoughtless and insensitive. Because ALS slurs her speech, people assume she is either drunk or has had a stroke. "When you're out," Denise says, "people tend to gravitate to the one who is not ill and ignore the sick person. This is how people respond to me, even though I always will be mentally intact." She tells Cohen she imagines people saying, "You are not normal, so I do not need to communicate with you. You are not worthy of my time."

"People say that?" Cohen asks her.

"No," she replies. "I see their faces. And they turn away."[1]

Denise's experience proves that not much has changed since biblical times, when, as we have seen, the "pollution" of sickness caused people to be isolated and rejected. That is why Jesus' ministry to the sick always coupled curing disease with healing the illness of social isolation and hopelessness. In doing so, Jesus provided a model for the kind of spiritual commitment needed to be one of God's conduits for healing.

§

Religion and Spirituality

It's common for people today to make a distinction between religion and spirituality. During the years I worked as a pastor I often heard comments such as, "I don't belong to an organized religion, but I'm very spiritual," or, "I don't go to synagogue, but I am a spiritual person," or, "The church focuses on doctrine, but I want to focus on spirituality." But I believe this is a false dichotomy. Just as a brain cannot live without a body or a body without a brain, religion cannot survive without spirituality and, for a Christian, spirituality cannot be sustained without religion. From earliest times, Christians have insisted that spiritual life cannot flourish without organized religion, or vital religion without passionate spirituality. To our Christian forebears, faith was not merely a personal quest, but a communal witness to the mighty acts of God in history, especially as manifest in the life, death, and resurrection of Jesus Christ.

As I see it, spirituality without religion is feeling without sacrifice, experience without discipleship. In one of the best known stories in Scripture (Luke 18:18-25), the rich ruler is convinced that he is spiritually worthy of eternal life because he has scrupulously kept all Ten Commandments. But Jesus tells him that he still lacks one thing: "Sell all that you own and distribute the money to the poor, and you will have treasure in heaven; then come, follow me." Notice that Jesus requires the young noble to share his wealth with others (sacrifice) and join Jesus in His work (discipleship); in other words, move from private, self-sufficient spirituality to an engagement with others in community and sacrificial living—the earmarks of sound religion. Biblically authentic spirituality requires the discipline of accountability within a believing community. In both the kinship culture of the Hebrews and the communal fervor of the early Church, it was understood that one could not worship God or enjoy the spiritual life in isolation from like believers. The contrast with modern Western culture could not be more dramatic. Our tendency today to reject organized religion in favor of spirituality is a legacy of modern-day democracy, capitalism, and individualism, along with a perception that religion is irrelevant to the intractable problems of our time.

I do not mean to suggest that one cannot have a moving experience of God outside of a church, because quite the opposite is true. For instance, people in all times and cultures have had profoundly spiritual experiences while communing with nature. Men and women have encountered the Divine in the desert, in the mountains, or in a single flower. Charles S. Peirce, a scientist and philosopher of the late 19th and early 20th century, believed that if you looked at the stars for half an hour and simply allowed your feelings to flow unhindered, you would experience an overwhelming impression that a Supreme Being must be responsible for the universe. Today, our scientific knowledge of merging galaxies, exploding supernovas, and the sheer vastness of space has not diminished the power of the universe to inspire us with awe. On a moonless night, away from the lights of the city, I can gaze at the heavens from the dock of our family cottage on East Pond, Maine and clearly make out the Big Dipper, the Milky Way, and the belt of Orion. In these unforgettable moments, my spirit is deeply moved.

But while an individual spiritual quest—whether it be exploring the wilderness, the world of art, or a foreign culture or religion—can be highly rewarding, within the Christian community private spirituality is a planet orbiting the sun of church worship and fellowship. A believer's connection to God is indivisible from a relationship to the Church. Each member is an indispensable part of that body, yet the body is more than the sum of its parts—it is the body of Christ. As individuals, we may believe in and worship the God of Christ, but we cannot belong to the body of Christ in isolation. Indeed, the metaphor of a "body" indicates that being a Christian is not meant to be an ephemeral, nonmaterial experience. Whether you choose to participate in the fervent worship of a black congregation, the silent peace of a Friends meeting, the stillness of a retreat, or a foot-stomping, praise-shouting Pentecostal service, Christian spirituality is a journey that links individual believers with the procession of all believers throughout history. We are connected to all who have served (and continue to serve) the God of Abraham, Isaac, Jacob, and Jesus Christ. Our collective journey ends in the resurrection of the Church of all ages to "meet the Lord in the air" (I Thessalonians 4:13-17).

§

Spirituality and Empathy: Feeling as God Feels

People who have had a spiritual experience often talk of feeling "close" to God. Obviously, this spatial metaphor is not meant to indicate physical proximity to God, but to describe an intimate experience of God's presence. This feeling of closeness to God is one of the most powerful attractions of spirituality, but unfortunately it does not necessarily imply a deeper awareness of the mind of God. We know too well from human experience that physical proximity is not the same as emotional closeness. That requires empathy.

But a physician friend of mine once asked me, "Can empathy be taught?"

I believe it can, though not as a principle so much as a response to a profound awareness of other people's experience. The virtue of empathy develops gradually along with a deeper understanding of others' suffering and our common humanity. Empathy is attuning to the feelings of others, a powerful gift that is learned by listening with the heart as well as the ears. It comes from sharing at the deepest levels of human consciousness. Feeling what someone else feels draws us into a deep knowledge not only of a person, but of the issues that affect that person. Empathy allows us to enter into others' feelings about themselves and their place in the world, and it is a vital component of moral development. Martha Nussbaum, an American philosopher and ethicist, speaks of an "ethical crudeness" to a morality based only on general principles and regulations. Justice, she says, requires much more than following certain rules. To think deeply about ethical issues and cultivate moral virtue we must also focus on emotions.[2]

Such a focus is not for the fainthearted. When we open ourselves to the feelings of others, we risk being radically transformed ourselves. I know because that is what happened to me in the early 1960s when I was teaching in a religiously affiliated college in Massachusetts. The nation was in the grips of the Civil Rights movement, and there were deep stirrings on our campus as well. Our black students and faculty members began to express disappointment—even rage—that at a Christian college they were not afforded full understanding, acceptance, and respect. I had grown up in New York City and had had several black school friends, but I had to admit that this alone did not open me to what my black students and colleagues were experiencing in those turbulent times.

Fortunately, I had majored in English in college, and so had a deep trust in the power of stories to illuminate human experiences that were foreign to me, and to sensitize me to the feelings of others.

My first effort to read my way into empathy for the black experience was *Black like Me* by John Griffin, the account of a white man who darkened his skin with radiation treatments, then traveled by bus to the South posing as a black man. With shocking honesty, Griffin recounted that as soon as he looked in the mirror and saw a black face, his feelings about himself changed. He *felt* what it was like to be black: inferior and powerless. Griffin's narrative, while powerful, was merely an entering point for me. I went from there to stories filled with volcanic pain and rage, such as Ralph Ellison's *Invisible Man* and Eldridge Cleaver's *Soul on Ice*, both of which upended me psychologically and forcefully raised my consciousness to another level.

I began to ask my black students to tell me their own stories of growing up in a society where all the levers of power were controlled by whites, where the sting of subtle and blatant prejudice was inflicted on a daily basis. They helped me imagine the ways in which their experiences in American culture were utterly different from mine, and led me into a deeper imaginative experience of being an "invisible" man. It was, for me, the beginning of a moral and spiritual transformation.

Because our feelings are connected to our moral imaginations, when our feelings change our moral compasses must change as well. This is much different than merely acceding to a new set of rules, for our feelings and imagination inspire rather than require us to do what is right; we become different persons for the right reasons. Logic or law can *require* us to be generous to the suffering and oppressed, but only feelings and moral imagination can *inspire* us to care about what happens to them. This, I believe, is what Jesus was saying when he told us that real change and authentic discipleship must go beyond what we do to why we do it—in other words, to our feelings and motives.

Rabbi Abraham Joshua Heschel explores the relationship between morality, virtue, spirituality, and feelings in his celebrated book, *The Prophets*. In this passage, he describes the shocking message of the Hebrew prophets:

> What manner of man is the prophet? A student of philosophy who turns from the discourses of the great metaphysicians to the orations of the prophets may feel as if he were going from the realm of the sublime to an area of trivialities. Instead of dealing with the timeless issues of being and becoming, of matter and form, of definitions and demonstrations, he is thrown into orations about widows and orphans, about the corruption of judges and affairs of the market place. Instead of showing us a way through the elegant mansions of the mind, the prophets take us to the slums. . . .[3]

Heschel goes on to argue that to us, an act of injustice—cheating a business partner or exploiting a poor neighbor—is a mere moral lapse, but to the prophets, it is a disaster. To us, injustice is an injury to a person; to the prophets, it is a death-blow to existence. To us, an incident; to them, a threat to the moral underpinnings of the universe (Heschel, pp. 3-4).

According to Heschel, the prophet feels what God feels. His speech is "urging, alarming, forcing onward, as if the words gushed from the heart of God, seeking entrance to the heart and mind of man . . ." (Heschel, pp. 6,7). "An analysis of prophetic utterances shows that the fundamental experience of the prophet is a fellowship with the feelings of God, a *sympathy with the divine pathos*, a communion with the divine consciousness. . . . The prophet hears God's voice and feels His heart" (Heschel, p. 26 *passim*).

Sharing God's feelings about the oppression of the poor roused the prophets to unthinkable acts of courage, calling Israel's leaders to account for their sins against the poor, especially the widows and orphans for whom the prophets spoke on God's behalf. Speaking truth to power, they attacked the political and religious leaders whose inability to empathize with the poor led them to acts of depraved cruelty:

> And I said: Listen, you heads of Jacob and rulers of the house of Israel! Should you not know justice?—you who hate the good and love the evil, who tear the skin off my people, and the flesh off their bones; who eat the flesh of my people, flay their skin off them, break their bones in pieces,

and chop them up like meat in a kettle, like flesh
in a caldron (Micah 3:1-3).

The prophets made clear what God wants from his people:

> Is not this the fast that I choose, to loose the bonds
> of injustice, to undo the thongs of the yoke, to let
> the oppressed go free, and to break every yoke? Is it
> not to share your bread with the hungry, and bring
> the homeless poor into your house; when you see
> the naked, to cover them, and to hide yourself
> from your own kin? Then your light shall break
> forth like the dawn, and your *healing* [emphasis
> mine] shall spring up quickly . . . Isaiah 58:6-8a).

Unfortunately for us, theology has traditionally been
more concerned with thinking God's thoughts than feeling
God's feelings. Searching the mind of God is an important
occupation for the Church and for the development of a spiritual life. But limiting spirituality to thinking as God thinks
(and thus focusing mainly on doctrines) is a legacy of Greek
rationalism, whose tools were logic and abstraction. Feeling
as God feels, while it does not exclude the rational, focuses
on God's passion for truth, justice, and righteousness and the
action that passion creates. The God of the Bible is a God
who acts, not just a God who thinks or "beholds the ideal
forms," as Plato might have described him. By the time of
St. Augustine, God was seen as perfect and impassible, unaffected and unlimited by what human beings say or do. This

long-held view of the nature of God, a view allied with Greek or Hellenic thought, is under attack today from Christians who argue for an "open" view of God rather than the closed one that has dominated Christian thought for millennia. The open view of God insists, as does Heschel, that God feels and reacts to human suffering and action.[4]

Christianity would be radically transformed if we habitually felt God's passion for people, especially the poor and oppressed, the sick and dying. And Christian healthcare would be transformed if we understood spirituality to embrace not only acts such as prayer and compassionate treatment, but also the capacity to feel the way God feels. Patients, their families, healthcare employees, community leaders, and everyone involved in healthcare would be affected. This is a formidable challenge, so let's look further at the steps we must take to feel as God feels for patients, their families, and their caregivers.

§

Feeling Our Woundedness

A human being does not come off an assembly line like a car or a cookie. We're all born uniquely, always genetically flawed, raised by imperfect families who function in a broken world. We are wounded from the beginning, and our wounds often deepen as we go through life. Spirituality begins with an awareness of this "illness" in our deepest selves. Self-consciousness is a uniquely human ability. "I" can think about "me" as if I were thinking about someone else, and there is nothing more concrete and personal than being the object of my own analysis. Self-consciousness inevitably leads to an awareness of our own imperfections. It forces us to see that we have disappointed the people who love us. We become conscious of a void we want to fill, a guilt we'd like to erase, a loss of meaning that leaves us moribund, what conservative Christians call "original sin." Such feelings are an important first step, because spirituality teaches us to first accept and then to grow from our weaknesses and failures.

Spirituality is discovered in that space between the paradoxical extremes of our woundedness and our desire for healing. It begins with the acceptance that our fractured beings, our imperfections, simply *are*. It is easy to ignore our flaws, but we ultimately must face them. We can try to deny our finitude and limitations.[5] We can try to make ourselves the center of the universe, with everyone and everything orbiting around us, grasping for power over others to escape our own limitations. But the process of spiritual growth helps us first to see, then to understand, and eventually to accept the imperfection that lies at the very core of our human *be*-ing.[6] It's a long and arduous process, but it is the first step toward change.

The philosopher and psychologist William James suggested that spirituality leads us to experience "torn-to-pieces-hood" (Kurtz, pp. 2-3). The spirituality of imperfection "speaks to both the inevitability of pain and the possibility of healing *within* the pain."[7] Confronted with his sin and imperfection, the psalmist declared:

Have mercy on me, O God,
according to your steadfast love;

according to your abundant mercy
blot out my transgressions.

Wash me thoroughly from my iniquity,
and cleanse me from my sin.

For I know my transgressions,
and my sin is ever before me . .

Create in me a clean heart, O God,
and put a new and right spirit
within me.

Do not cast me away from your presence
and do not take your holy spirit from me (Ps. 51,
passim).

From the time we are born, our self-image is shaped by the way others see us. Well into adulthood, and perhaps for the rest of our lives, most of us will view ourselves through the eyes of our parents and other authority figures from our childhood. If we are loved by our parents and grandparents, we will learn how to love others as well as ourselves. Our emotional and spiritual health is nourished by the conviction that the people we admire and love most believe deeply in our value, potential, and lovability. That is why child psychologists warn parents never to call children lazy, stupid, or useless. Children internalize those parental perceptions, and once they *believe* those perceptions, they will *become* them to a degree they may not recognize until they are grown. If when we are young our parents treat us as people whose opinions deserve to be heard, whose mistakes are quickly forgiven, whose mere presence in the world is cherished, then we too will see ourselves as good and worthy.

At least until they are adolescents, children think of their parents as almost inerrant and omniscient. What their parents say is simply what is; what their parents do is the way things should be done. Young children are incapable of objective, realistic assessments of parental behavior. If their parents mistreat them, children will usually assume that they are bad and deserve mistreatment. To believe their parents are deeply flawed would destroy their sense of a secure and rational world. Raised without love, children would rather believe they are unlovable than that their parents are unloving. As psychiatrist M. Scott Peck observes, whenever there is a major deficit in parental love, the child will, in all likelihood, respond to that deficit by assuming they are the cause of the deficit, thereby developing an unrealistically negative self-image.[8]

How we feel about ourselves can also be influenced by our experiences in church. Does the preacher makes us feel worthy of God's love and salvation? Are we included in church activities and leadership? When I was pastor of a large congregation, a new member told me that church day was the loneliest day of her week. Her husband was not a believer, so she attended church alone. When other members didn't seem to recognize her loneliness, she began to wonder if the problem was with her. Another woman told me that her mother had had such rigid ideas about keeping the sabbath day that she and her sisters were forced to spend all morning in church and the entire afternoon reading the Bible. As she grew up, she never felt good enough, never capable of pleasing either her mother or God. The promises of the gospel that in Christ she was infinitely pleasing to God simply fell on deaf ears. She did not *feel* loved or forgiven by God. She read the words of the Bible but insisted they did not apply to her. It was difficult—if not impossible—for her to feel the way God felt about her. She was trapped in an emotional cage.

Self-loathing is not limited to the influence of family and church, but can be systematized in social constructs such as racism. We too easily believe what others perceive in us and are not able to readily understand that their distorted vision of us may reflect their inadequacies far more than ours. Throughout our lives, this powerful dynamic may diminish, but it never disappears. In adulthood, if we believe other people like us, we see ourselves as likable; if we believe others view us as attractive and successful, we feel attractive and successful. This is why spirituality must begin with an awareness of how we feel about ourselves and why we feel the way we do. We should also ask ourselves how we feel others view us and whether we should give validity to their perceptions. Finally, we should ask how God perceives us. It may be that the believer's deepest self-understanding begins with the discovery that the perceptions of the God who made us are more trustworthy than our own. The way God sees us often contradicts the way we see ourselves as well as the way others see us. Our self-perception may have been shaped by early experiences with parents and authority figures, but it must be reshaped by our knowledge of how God feels about us if we are to experience authentic Christian spirituality.

§

How God Feels About Us

If feeling our own woundedness is the first step in spiritual growth, the second step is to feel the way God feels about us. For those who never take this step, the results can be tragic. When I was growing up in Brooklyn, I had a friend whose parents had separated. Perhaps to compensate for the absence of a father, my friend tried desperately to be popular with older boys in the neighborhood. At first he was thrilled when these fellows let him hang out with them, but soon they began to take advantage of his loneliness and vulnerability in the cruelest possible way. They started to abuse him sexually. As a result, this boy was filled with shame and a visceral fear of being around people that crippled him for the rest of his life. The only relief from his inner pain came in solitary pursuits such as drinking and gambling. He loathed himself for no other reason than that he had internalized the perceptions of people who were ultimately unworthy of his regard. His self-loathing had nothing to do with the truth about his true self, the truth as God saw it. He was a victimized child of God, capable of accomplishing much if only he could see himself as God saw him, feel about himself the way God felt about him. God saw what he could become if evil had not polluted his capacity for hope and trust. His self-hatred could only be overcome by an experience of God's loving acceptance, mediated by others who had experienced it for themselves.

God's compassion for us is boundless. He offers us a new vision of ourselves, but we must trust what the Bible tells us about God's love for us. In God's name, Jesus Christ loved people so absolutely that he gave them the power to change the way they felt about themselves. His affirmation of their value, of their right to be accepted into society through the gospel's proclamation that their sins had been forgiven, was life-changing. Once they realized how Jesus saw them, *they wanted to become the person he saw.* The poor, prostitutes, thieves, and even rich, traitorous tax collectors followed him faithfully because he taught them to see themselves through the eyes of God, to feel what God felt about them, and to know that they were *not* outside God's forgiveness and redemption.

The way Jesus treated people took them by surprise. They understood by how Jesus made them feel that he saw them very differently than they saw themselves. He even helped the despised, socially isolated, crooked tax-collector Levi-Matthew, who was no doubt filled with self-loathing, to see himself as someone of infinite importance. There is no other explanation for why Matthew would leave his former life to become a faithful apostle. Jesus invited people to see themselves not through eyes of judgment and condemnation, but through eyes of forgiveness and infinite possibility. What a gift—to see ourselves as we can be, as we are meant to be through God's grace and not simply as we think we are. That is one of the things Jesus meant when he said: "I have come that they might have life, and have it more abundantly" (John 10:10). What faith brings to this dynamic is the power to believe that the wisest, most loving reality in the universe sees us more truly than we or anyone else can see us; that God sees the best that we are and the best that we can be.

Spirituality, then, is a two-step process. In the first step our glimpse of God's goodness leads us to acknowledge our imperfections; the next step is the gift of seeing ourselves as redeemed, renewed, mature, and complete in Christ's righteousness. Feeling the way God feels about us provides the spiritual balance between self-conceit and self-loathing. This process of knowing ourselves as God knows us is long and arduous. That is why discipleship and sanctification, which both involve growing in likeness to Christ, take a lifetime.

Many today who suffer from low self-esteem turn to psychotherapy, and it is true that a competent professional can provide real relief. But as a Christian, I believe that while therapy can be invaluable in some circumstances, it cannot give us the deepest, truest picture of who we are. Our Western focus on individualism is a natural outgrowth of Socrates' dictum to "know thyself," but self-knowledge is impossible without God, because we, being made in the image of God, need to know God in order to know ourselves. The Bible does not teach that to know God we must first know ourselves, but that if we would know ourselves, we must first know God, for God's vision of who we are is truer than our vision of ourselves. We must believe that God believes in us. We must forgive ourselves because God has forgiven us. The apostle John reminds us that "we love him because he first loved us" (I John 4:19).

To the woman caught in adultery, Jesus said: "Neither do I condemn you. Go your way, and from now on do not sin again" (John 8:11b). Jesus saw this woman as capable of much more than the behavior she was trapped in. Only when she trusted that the way Jesus saw her was more real than how she saw herself could she begin to see herself as someone who could turn her life around. Jesus' compassion for her was so powerful that I can believe she grew into one of his most courageous and faithful disciples.

§

The Wounded Can Become Healers

Any kind of vulnerability creates a spiritual crisis that prompts us to reach out to God. This is why it is so important for healthcare professionals to understand that a health crisis is almost always a physical *and* spiritual crisis. A threat to our health or a brush with death poses a serious challenge to our humanity and dignity. It turns us into what Arthur W. Frank has aptly called "wounded storytellers," whose life stories are so disrupted they must be rewritten to incorporate new realities.[9] My son's father-in-law has added an astonishing new chapter to his life since his devastating stroke. He and his wife now operate a horse farm for disabled children, where interaction with these magnificent animals helps to heal the children's loss of self-esteem. It is difficult work, but they have discovered that by healing others, they experience their own healing.

In the previous chapter I referred to Joseph Cardinal Bernardin's experience as he faced death and how he found meaning and peace by reaching out to others. Bernardin observed in his book *The Gift of Peace*[10] that it is well for Christians to do their praying and spiritual work before their bodies deteriorate and leave little strength for doing so. At the same time, he felt compelled, once he finished chemotherapy, to go into the cancer wards and visit the patients. The gift of peace he enjoyed had to be shared. Counseling and praying with other cancer victims, he felt, was to be the final ministry of his life. Committing himself to the spiritual healing of others helped to heal him as he neared the end of his life.

Richard Cohen cites the case of Sarah, who lives with Crohn's disease. She is ill at ease with people she doesn't know well because they don't realize how sick she can get quite unexpectedly. Since Crohn's disease particularly challenges the digestive tract, it's no wonder Sarah is uncomfortable in social situations. "Let them feel what it is like to desperately need a nap by two every day," she says. "They can swallow sixty pills a day or be on those steroids. Let them see what that does to your psyche." Cohen observes that "self-absorption is emblematic of chronic illness. We become hyperaware of our long siege. Sometimes that is all we can see. And although we will not admit this, sometimes we do feel sorry for ourselves. . . . Sarah wants badly to say the right things and project a calm resolve. Yet knowing that the strong face she shows the world is only a dream suggests how alone she can feel" (Cohen, pp. 211-212).

Wounded storytellers need to be heard because their suffering has upended their self-sufficiency. They want to make a difference in the world before it is too late and telling the story of who they are now, in their illness, contributes to their healing and helps them face an uncertain future. Morrie Schwartz, the dying professor profiled in *Tuesdays with Morrie*,[11] felt compelled to talk about the importance of living a life filled with friends, family, community, and a sense of contributing to the betterment of society. Showing us how to live as we die was his way of leaving a blessing behind, of giving meaning to the meaninglessness of disease and death. And there are countless other wounded who have sought healing by helping others. After he was diagnosed with Parkinsonism, Michael J. Fox retired from acting to devote his life to eradicating this dread disease. Christopher Reeve, paralyzed by a fall from a horse, gave his remaining days to finding a cure for catastrophic spinal cord injuries. Both men discovered that, while they might not live to see a cure for themselves, their work to fund research that would benefit succeeding generations would give meaning to their personal struggles.

In the same way that patients can be transformed into healers, those who love them, and who remain to grieve when attempts at a cure fail, can also become wounded healers. When I was teaching college in New England I had a freshman student who planned to enter the ministry when he finished college. Tall, good-looking, and bright, he was one of the most promising students in his class. Not long into his first semester, he took time off to undergo a series of medical tests near his home in Connecticut. To everyone's dismay, he was diagnosed with leukemia and began treatment. We all hoped and prayed for his recovery, but all reports were that his prognosis was poor. I traveled to Connecticut to visit the young man in the hospital, accompanied by his pastor. I was not as experienced in ministering to the sick in those days, and the sight of my student jarred me. He was thin and severely jaundiced. Between labored breaths he looked up at me and said, "If this . . . is what it takes . . . to get well . . . I don't think . . . I can do it much longer."

After a short time, the pastor suggested that we go buy oil for an anointing, as counseled in the epistle of James. We were gone only fifteen minutes, but when we returned to the student's hospital room, his bed was empty. Bewildered by this, we stopped a nurse in the hall and asked if the young man had been moved to another room. With tears in her eyes, she told us he had died while we were on our errand. Suddenly I became light-headed and felt like I had been punched in the stomach. I was unprepared to lose such a promising student—one not much younger than I was—let alone virtually witness his death. (Experience has since taught me that people generally know when they are dying, and that we should learn to be sensitive to their signals.)

The pastor and I found the student's distraught parents and siblings in the hospital waiting room and took them home, where the parents laid plans that very day to honor their son's memory with a college scholarship fund in his name. For years afterward, at each annual awards assembly, their son's young life was honored as some deserving student received funds to help pay for their education, a generous act that was the grieving parents' way of bringing about their own healing.

This pattern is played out on a larger scale as well. When Candy Lightner lost her 13-year-old daughter Cari to a drunk driver, she channeled her rage and grief into founding Mothers Against Drunk Driving (MADD). From her tragedy, she launched a remarkable effort to educate, inform, and change permissive attitudes toward drinking and driving. Today MADD's influence is pervasive, with chapters in all 50 states and many international affiliates. Candy Lightner acted in a way that brought healing to society and, I suspect, to herself. What she did was in the spirit of the healing ministry of Jesus, a spiritual effort to implement God's passion for relieving human suffering.

§

The Spiritual Mission of Wounded Caregivers

While the woundedness of a patient is obvious, woundedness in a caregiver is not. As wounded healers, the best physicians, nurses, and caregivers are themselves healed as they cure and heal their patients. Necessarily trained to minimize identifying with their patients' suffering (no one wants a weeping surgeon), many admit they are nonetheless unable to completely disengage their natural human empathy. This poses a particular challenge to doctors whose specialties require them to frequently deliver bad news to patients and their families. They report that the experience is always gut-wrenching, and that they never get so hardened that it does not haunt them. In the powerful chronicle of her training and practice as a surgeon, *Final Exam: A Surgeon's Reflections on Mortality*, [12] Pauline Chen recounts that despite her best efforts she was unable to ignore her own suffering over losing a patient. For this reason, caregivers suffer high rates of burnout from what some call "compassion fatigue." For many, the needless suffering and death caused by a healthcare system forced to focus more on the bottom line than on individual patients is a cause for frustration and guilt. Others suffer the moral distress of knowing the right thing to do while being constrained by law or policy from doing it. For still others, patient care has become a job, not the vocation or ministry they hoped for. The healthcare system's insistence on efficiency often limits patient interaction to largely medical issues. Practitioners feel robbed of the personal connection to patients they used to enjoy and that used to foster two-way healing. Their exhausting work often obscures God's presence. Nurses are seldom able to hold a patient's hand in the middle of the night and spend an hour just talking about the patient's fears for their future, yet this ministry is what they and their patients both crave.

If Christian healthcare institutions and caregivers would rediscover how God feels about the work they do, it would reenergize their enthusiasm for their tasks. Just as infrared lenses allow us to see in the dark, healthcare workers and caregivers at home need to see in themselves and in their patients what God sees. Institutional leaders and administrators are uniquely positioned to foster this process of self-understanding in the people they employ by committing themselves to seeing their caregivers as God sees them. For this to happen, both groups must listen intently and refrain from talking past each other. Then administrators can take the lead in bringing spirituality back into healthcare, not simply by offering prayers and devotionals before meetings, but by the ordinary, daily business of helping the people they employ to see themselves through God's eyes. How is this done? By loving them as God loves them, by caring for and about them even as they care for and about their patients.

You may ask, "So if spirituality boils down to the ordinary act of loving other people, how do I go about it? How do I show love to my patients? To my employees?" As is so often the case, children seem to be way ahead of us in this regard. A teacher friend of mine e-mailed me an account of a classroom exercise in which a group of 4- to 8-year-olds was asked, "What does love mean?" Their childish wisdom may astonish you:

➤ When my grandma got arthritis she couldn't bend over and paint her toenails anymore. So my grandpa does it for her all the time, even when his hands got arthritis too. That's love. Rebecca, age 8

➤ Love is when you go out to eat and give somebody most of your French fries without making them give you any of theirs. Chrissy, age 6

➤ Love is when my Mommy makes coffee for my Daddy and she takes a sip before giving it to him, to make sure the taste is okay. Danny, age 7

➤ Love is what's in the room with you at Christmas if you stop opening presents and listen. Bobby, age 7

➤ My Mommy loves me more than anybody. You don't see anyone else kissing me to sleep at night. Clare, age 6

➤ Love is when Mommy sees Daddy and says he is still more handsome than Robert Redford. Joanne, age 6

Finally, author and lecturer Leo Buscaglia once judged a contest to find the most caring child. The winner was a 4-year-old whose next-door neighbor was an elderly gentleman who had recently lost his wife. As Buscaglia tells it, "Upon seeing the man cry, the little boy went into the old gentleman's yard, climbed onto his lap, and just sat there. When his mother asked what he had said to the neighbor, the little boy said, 'Nothing, I just helped him cry.'"

What can these children, who don't have the same internal barriers to honest emotional expression that adults do, teach us about how to practice this kind of spontaneous, unself-conscious love in a hospital setting? What does their thoughtfulness tell us love should be like in a doctor's office, a clinic, a nursing home or even a private home? Can you imagine they might say something like the following?

> ➤ Love is cleaning up the mess my grandpa made when he didn't quite get to the bathroom in time.

> ➤ Love is what makes my exhausted mom smile at her fellow nurses at 3 a.m. in the morning.

> ➤ When my grandma had Alzheimer's and was afraid of everything, love is what made the doctors and nurses speak softly and touch her tenderly.

> ➤ Love is holding a dying patient's hand in the middle of the night as long as he needs you.

> ➤ Love is the doctor coming back after a busy day just to see how the patient is doing.

Let's go a step further and imagine the behavior of leaders who treasure the love of God as they implement policies in their faith-based institutions:

➤ Love is transparency and honesty within the institution about its strengths and weaknesses;

➤ Love is openly communicating important values and information to your employees through:

- ► Town hall meetings

- ► Paycheck news sheets and monthly newsletters mailed to employees' homes

- ► Regular departmental meetings to review the level of care provided in specific cases

- ► Prayer and devotionals before committee and board meetings

- ► Annual or biannual weekend conferences to review the hospital's mission

- ► The way you listen to them

➤ Love is encouraging employees to communicate their concerns to you through:

- ► Confidential "grapevine" or "hotline" networks provided via phone or intranet that guarantee anonymity and protection from reprisal

- ► An employee assistance program that provides an advocate with management when needed, through human resource and chaplain personnel

- ► Acting on what you learn

- Love is creating flexible, family-friendly human resource policies, whether required by law or not, that cover:

  - Family medical leave

  - Expectant parents

  - Retirement benefits

  - Paid time-off policies that allow employees to help each other in an emergency

  - Severance policies that are fair and embody due process

  - Promotion from within as much as possible

- Love is creating a leadership and employee development program that helps loyal workers advance in their professions.

- Love is employees giving tens of thousands of dollars each year, as well as paid time off, to help fellow employees under financial stress care for their sick children at home.

- Love is giving Thanksgiving and Christmas baskets to employees and community members who will have no holiday without them.

- Love is working hard to create a culture of spirituality and integrity that makes employees better people.

> ➤ Love is giving appropriate hope to dying patients assaulted by fear.

> ➤ Love is being fiscally responsible so we can continue to provide quality care to the community.

> ➤ Love is finding donors and giving them the opportunity to support worthy charities for their neighbors.

> ➤ Love is dealing with employees openly, honestly, and sensitively, and apologizing and making amends when you don't.

> ➤ Love is maintaining excellence in whatever responsibility is entrusted to you.

Being a spiritually committed enterprise is all this and more.

It has been my good fortune to work for the Kettering Healthcare Network, a faith-based healthcare system that conscientiously tries to do all the things listed above and succeeds to a remarkable degree. One of my new hires told me after only a few months that she had never seen an organization as generous with its employees. Another long-time employee told me that she had been working at Kettering Hospital only a short time when her husband committed suicide. Right away, not only her own department but the whole organization rallied to help her. The Employee Assistance Fund, made up entirely of employee donations, provided thousands of dollars to help her maintain her mortgage payments until she could recover financially, while fellow employees donated paid time-off hours so she could attend to her affairs without losing pay. "This is my family, not just my place of work," she told me, articulating the ethos that must define every faith-based institution.

§

Empathy in the Gospels

We have seen that spirituality is a growing awareness that even in our imperfections we are loved by God. We have learned that to be truly spiritual we need to catch God's vision of who we are and to value ourselves as God values us. And we have seen that the spiritual challenge for caregivers in Christian hospitals is to feel the way God feels about their patients and their ministry to those patients. To fully grasp these insights, we must look more deeply into the gospel message.

Some may object to thinking about the gospel in terms of feelings and say: "I thought the gospel was not about feeling but about choosing to accept Christ as my savior and to embody God's *agape* love. When Jesus said in the Sermon on the Mount that I must love my enemies and pray for those who persecute me (Matthew 5:43-48), he was not telling me to *feel* love for them but to *act* consistently for their good. He meant that I should not give in to feelings of revenge or retaliation. So if I just treat my enemy with respect, am I not obeying Jesus' command to love even if I still despise my enemy?" The answer is yes and no.

Certainly, any commitment to abandon revenge against an enemy goes a long way toward fulfilling Christ's intention. It breaks the cycle of violence caused by endless retaliation. But, is that all there is to God's *agape* love? Didn't Jesus also teach us in that same Sermon on the Mount that his commandments go beyond our behavior to our motives and deepest feelings? We are not just to abhor injuring another, we are to despise the feelings of hatred, revenge, anger, lust, and covetousness that lead to it. "You have heard that it was said to those of ancient times, 'You shall not murder'; and 'whoever murders shall be liable to judgment.' But I say to you that if you are angry with a brother or sister, you will be liable to judgment . . . . You have heard that it was said, 'You shall not commit adultery.' But I say to you that everyone who looks at a woman with lust has already committed adultery with her in his heart" (Matthew 5:21-22a; 27-28). Jesus challenges us not merely to repudiate revenge, but to let go of the anger that fuels it. Forgiving my enemy goes to the core of how I feel about him, for feelings are like fuel that stoke the "habits of the heart" that Robert Bellah writes about.[13]

The Hebrew philosophy underlying Christian theology does not separate thinking, feeling, and acting because it does not see a human being as an immortal spirit residing within a mortal body—only a unified, complex individual. When Pope John Paul II forgave Mehmet Ali Ağca for attempting to assassinate him, I suspect that he did not mouth the words of forgiveness while inwardly feeling rage, but that he felt sincere compassion for his would-be killer. Years ago I saw a television report about a pastor who believed the gospel required him to forgive his daughter's rapist-murderer. He felt that the only way to do this was to regularly visit the man in prison, where he could see him in his humanity. But the pastor's efforts to help and even be reconciled with his daughter's killer were more than his wife could bear, and she finally divorced him. Unlike her husband, she could not let go of her hatred of the man who had viciously ended her daughter's life. (I offer this story as an illustration of two different responses to Christ's teaching on compassion, not as a judgment of the mother, whose suffering must have been unspeakable.)

Christian compassion is awakened by learning to feel the suffering of others, either by direct interaction or through the imaginative power of stories. Willing ourselves into caring for them (a dubious prospect at best) will not do. Difficult as it may be, victims of crime have testified that it is possible to feel the suffering of the perpetrator. Even Jesus, while dying on the cross, prayed for his killers: "Father, forgive them, for they know not what they do." Most of us have little sense of what lies behind a violent personality. Unless we have witnessed their physical abuse by malicious parents or felt their frustration within a hopeless poverty, we need to remember John Wesley's observation when he saw a drunk lying in the gutter: "There, but for the grace of God, go I."

§

To Know God's Heart

I hope I have made clear by now my belief that an essential element of Christian spirituality is a growing capacity to empathize with others and to feel what God feels about the desolation caused by sin. How does God feel about crumbling cultural values? About adultery, promiscuity, and greed? About our abandonment of the homeless and the mentally ill? How does God feel about our irrational consumption of Earth's resources? And most importantly for a caregiver, how does God feel about my patients and me?

Too many Christians believe that God does not truly love or care about them. They've lost any capacity to feel the way God feels about them. In a cruel paradox, church services and Christian fellowship sometimes exacerbate their feelings of isolation from God. Breaking through that wall of doubt—that chasm between hearing God's words of love and acceptance, and believing they apply to us—is a profound challenge. Believing that God feels compassion for us is far more empowering to the Christian life than believing God's experience is untouched by our need. As we all know, addicts are most impacted by interventions in which their family's anguish directly confronts them. The addict needs to *feel* their torment and love.

The purpose of spiritual exercises such as worship, prayer, meditation, Bible study, and service is not merely to draw us closer to God, but to sensitize us to feel God's feelings. Knowing the truth is more than knowing God's mind; it is knowing God's heart, as far as that is possible. It is this spiritual awareness that propels us into the world's suffering and the church's proclamation of the gospel. Many evangelists have a passion for soul-winning because they feel the Good Shepherd's anxiety over the one lost sheep. They have caught God's passion. The God who feels our suffering and our fear of separation from the Shepherd is a wounded God, and we his servants feel the divine anguish.

How do we learn to feel what God feels? The same way we learn to feel the humiliation of poverty or racism: through the stories, parables, sermons, letters, poetry, and proverbs of Scripture, and especially through the story of Jesus. We also learn to feel what God feels through the worship and preaching of the church. It's no different than how a white person learns to feel the harshness of racism. When you read the covenant God made with Israel in the book of Deuteronomy, and then read the book of Amos, you realize just how far the Hebrews had strayed from that covenant by the 8th century BCE. By failing to care for the poor, they had violated God's will, and their unfaithfulness is likened to adultery. Hosea uses the same metaphor to describe what Israel has done. Like Hosea, who went out night after night to reclaim his wife from the bed of another lover, God never stops trying to reclaim his own. That living parable helped the Hebrews *feel* God's sorrow over them.[14]

How can someone in the healthcare profession translate this truth to the workplace? Spirituality in healthcare involves many of the things we've already discussed, such as helping patients heal in the midst of illness and ministering to them as whole persons, not just sick bodies. But I believe it must also include learning how God feels about the sick and suffering through either direct personal experience or the power of enlightened imagination.

We've all seen television footage chronicling the cycles of oppression and brutality in many of the world's developing nations. We've witnessed, from a safe distance, endless racial and economic disputes and the famine and refugees they leave in their wake. One evening, unable to endure any longer the faces of displaced women and children who might easily die between commercials for cars and hamburgers, I stepped away from the television and looked outside at a lush green world where food was plentiful and no armed bandits were stealing it from those who needed it most. On the newscast, the announcer was discussing the political, military, and socioeconomic aspects of the catastrophe, but I was concerned about the theological meaning of these events and how they should affect my work in Christian healthcare.

According to the Bible, even those people suffering and dying a world away are my brothers and sisters. God's love for them and for us compels us to help them however we can. In doing so, we open ourselves to an immeasurable blessing. They are the "least of these," the ones for whom Christ feels so strong a kinship that a cup of water or a loaf of bread given to them becomes a cup or loaf offered to him.

When the Son of Man comes in his glory, and all the angels with him, then he will sit on the throne of his glory. All the nations will be gathered before him, and he will separate people from one another as a shepherd separates the sheep from the goats, and he will put the sheep at his right hand and the goats at the left. Then the king will say to those at his right hand, "Come you that are blessed by my Father, inherit the kingdom prepared for you from the foundation of the world; for I was hungry and you gave me food, I was thirsty and you gave me something to drink, I was a stranger and you welcomed me, I was naked and you gave me clothing, I was sick and you took care of me, I was in prison and you visited me." Then the righteous will answer him, "Lord, when was it that we saw you hungry and gave you food, or thirsty and gave you something to drink? And when was it that we saw you a stranger and welcomed you, or naked and gave you clothing? And when was it that we saw you sick or in prison and visited you?" And the king will answer them, "Truly I tell you, *just as you did it to one of the least of these who are members of my family, you did it to me*" [emphasis mine] (Matthew 25:31-40).

To draw near to those who suffer is to draw near to Christ and to feel Christ draw near to us. This is a two-way interaction that requires turning feelings into actions. We cannot do nothing and feel the suffering of others, just as we cannot feel the suffering of others and do nothing. Seeing televised reports is only the first step. Spirituality requires us to touch sufferers. We must be in a hospital room, hospice, homeless shelter, soup kitchen, or refugee camp. We must look in the eyes of those who need healing and feel privileged to be serving them and Jesus in them. In the hospital where I worked as an administrator, those not involved in clinical care were expected to "walk in a nurse's shoes" from time to time. Whether an executive or a trustee, we were to work with the professionals in caring for their patients. On one of my walks, I was asked to help bathe an elderly man afflicted with Alzheimer's disease. A tall, striking man who might once have been a leader in the community, he was now virtually helpless. As I worked with the nurse, I was struck by the truth that what she did for her patients was sacred. Her touch, like the touch of Jesus on the sick of Palestine, was holy. In that smelly room, I was made aware that the patient's ailing body was a dwelling for God's Spirit. I had an epiphany—an overpowering sense of God's presence and grace—and I was blessed. That blessing healed me in ways I cannot express. This is not to say that there is any value in suffering, only to say that God is always with those who suffer. As Matthew chapter 25 reminds us, to touch them is to touch—and be touched by—God. To effect their healing is to be healed.

Sickness and death are spiritual nightmares that make us question the meaning of life and the compassion of God. As playwright Tony Kushner prayed on World AIDS Day, "Must grace fall so unevenly on the earth?" A body can be sick, but only a life can be ill, and when you or someone you love is ill, you require healing at every level of your being. The spirituality that leads to this kind of healing begins with recognizing our imperfections and accepting our need for God, a need intensified by sickness and suffering. Spirituality then evolves into knowing God wants us to be joyful and free of the suffering caused by poverty, oppression, guilt, and sickness. This awareness helps us to feel God's compassion for the sick and oppressed who are separated from their rightful joy of life.

Today, nursing students may be offered a single course on the ethics of healthcare, while medical students rarely are required to take a similar course. But all caregivers concerned about the relationship between spirituality and healing must continually ask: How does God feel about the suffering of my patients? How does God feel about the way we treat our patients and the way caregivers and those who support them treat each other? How does God feel about the way management and employees interact with each other? All healthcare entities that identify their mission as Christian need to shape their training, hiring policies, and corporate culture toward helping their employees feel as God feels about their patients and their coworkers. A true revolution in Christian healthcare would result in patients experiencing the person of Jesus in the care they receive at our hands. Anything less cannot claim to be an heir to Christ's healing ministry.

Notes and References

¹Cohen, Richard M. *Strong at the Broken Places: Voices of Illness, a Chorus of Hope* (New York: Harper Collins, 2008), 29-31, passim.

²Nussbaum, Martha. *Love's Knowledge: Essays on Philosophy and Literature* (New York: Oxford University Press, 1990), 3-51, passim.

³Heschel, Abraham Joshua. *The Prophets* (New York: Harper's, 1962), 3.

⁴Pinnock, Clark, Richard Rice, John Sanders, and William Hasker. *The Openness of God: A Biblical Challenge to the Traditional Understanding of God* (Downers Grove, IL: InterVarsity Press, 1994).

⁵Becker, Ernest. *The Denial of Death* (New York: Free Press Paperbacks, 1973).

⁶Kurtz, Ernest and Katherine Ketcham. *The Spirituality of Imperfection: Storytelling and the Journey to Wholeness* (New York: Bantam Books, 1992), 2.

⁷Chesterton, GK. *The Paradoxes of Mr. Pond* (Philadelphia: Dufor Editions, 1937), 55.

⁸Peck, M. Scott. *People of the Lie: The Hope for Healing Human Evil* (New York: Simon and Schuster, 1983), 60.

⁹Franks, Arthur W. *The Wounded Storyteller: Body, Illness and Ethics* (Chicago: University of Chicago Press, 1995).

[10]Bernardin, Joseph Cardinal. *The Gift of Peace* (New York: Double-day, 1997).

[11]Albom, Mitch. *Tuesdays with Morrie* (New York: Doubleday, 1997).

[12]Chen, Pauline E. *Final Exam: A Surgeon's Reflections on Mortality* (New York: Knopf, 2007), 108-116.

[13]Bellah, Robert, Richard Madsen, William M. Sullivan, Ann Swidler, and Steven M. Tipton. *Habits of the Heart: Individualism and Commitment in American Life* (Berkeley, CA: University of California Press, 1985).

[14]When Greek and Hebrew thought began to merge during the early Christian era, the Hebrew insight that God can feel was lost. More in line with Greek philosophy, God became changeless and therefore unaffected by events of this world, including its suffering.

God's Cure for Caregiver Burnout

Burnout: The Cost of Compassion

Whether they are believers or not, those committed to health-care know there simply is not enough time. Time, the "house" in which we seek to accomplish everything, is not spacious enough to fulfill the compassionate person's commitments. The week consists of a series of trade-offs between work, home, and self. More often than not, self receives the least amount of time because compassionate people do not feel guilty taking time away from themselves; they feel guilty taking time away from others. The virtue of self-denial quickly becomes a vehicle for self-destruction. As Quaker sociologist Parker J. Palmer wrote in his book *The Active Life: A Spirituality of Work, Creativity and Caring:*

> For some of us, the primary path to aliveness is the active life of work, creativity, and caring. The active life is an extraordinary blessing and curse. The blessing is obvious: . . . the active life makes it possible to discover ourselves and our world, to test and extend our powers, to connect with other beings, to co-create a common reality. . . . Take away the opportunity to work, to create, or to care . . . and you have deprived someone of the chance to feel fully human. But the active life also carries a curse. Many of us know what it is to live lives not of action but of frenzy, to go from day to day exhausted and unfulfilled by our attempts to work, create, and care. Many of us know the violence of the active life. . . . Action poses some of our deepest spiritual crises as well as some of our most heartfelt joy.[1]

Clearly, many in the health professions work grueling hours from a compelling drive to make more money, publish in another peer-reviewed journal, or win a lucrative research grant. But for most of the healthcare workers I know, concern for their patients, not making more money or being more notable, is what compels them to work excessively. For them, the most dangerous cause of burnout is their virtues, not their weaknesses, and they are particularly susceptible to what might be called the "virtue dilemma," which can become the shortest route to burnout. These compassionate individuals became caregivers out of a deep desire to ease the suffering of others, to address issues from their own wounded childhoods, to deal with their own fear of death, or from a commitment to Jesus as the "model healer." These factors impose on them an ethical imperative to heal the sick. They feel they "ought" to do this, that they are "called" to this service or ministry. Responding to this imperative can be a noble virtue, but one that more often than not leads to exhaustion and burnout. When that happens, how can these compassionate caregivers say to their patients, "Sorry, but I need to get home at a decent hour to get some rest"?

§

The Supererogatory/Compassion Temptation to Burnout
Compassion for their patients can tempt caregivers to embrace what ethicists call a supererogatory ethic, meaning a work ethic that goes beyond the requirements of duty. A supererogatory ethic, unlike one's professional obligations, is by definition limitless in its response to human need and can be brought on by draining, depleting compassion.

Some time ago I had lunch with a woman who was working with me as part of a group providing palliative care at the hospital where I was on staff. This program was a direct outgrowth of an enthusiastic response to Bill Moyers' PBS series "On Our Own Terms," which dealt with issues of death and dying. My colleague, a cancer survivor who had faced her own mortality, told me that her physician husband was spending a lot more time at home since his retirement a few months earlier. She had tried to interest him in watching tapes of the Moyers series with her, but he had adamantly refused. Frustrated by his reluctance, she had pressed him to explain. Looking into her eyes, he had said, "You have no idea how hard it is to deliver bad news to patients time and time again for thirty years. I'm sorry, but I just can't bear to watch those tapes."

My friend told me that this had surprised her, because her husband had never before expressed the inner pain that being a caregiver had caused him. Dr. Naomi Remen, however, has written of her discovery that even physicians who share a practice often do not share such personal burdens with each other. They may not even suspect that anyone else feels the way they do.[2]

Theologian Richard B. Steele points to the "double-sidedness" of compassion. It usually is involuntary, spontaneous, and uncontrived, a mark of one's "vulnerability to another person's distress. Indeed, genuine compassion seems to be something that is almost torn out of us by the grievous circumstances under which someone else lives."[3] But, Steele suggests, "there is a sense in which compassion is voluntary. Or at least it is a trait of character that we must intentionally cultivate and it typically grows in scope and intensity as we mature morally."[4] Compassion is a habit or disposition that cannot help but unfold in the caregiver unless it is consciously resisted. When one's life is dedicated to relieving the suffering of others, when the needs of others are the focus of one's daily efforts, one inevitably suffers along with the suffering. The need for balance, rest, and time with friends and family seems morally insignificant. Caregivers cannot help feeling that taking time away from service to others is self-indulgent. Thus, ironically, the very virtues that make for a good caregiver may contribute to self-destructive behavior. Caregivers of deep faith, especially, do not know how to say "yes" to their personal needs if that "yes" feels like a "no" to their needy patients or to what they believe God has called them to do. One Christian physician struggled to control his emotions as he described this inner conflict to me. Perversely, the religious imperative arising out of the ministry of Jesus can become a stumbling-block to self-preservation.

§

Temptations to Burnout

The "Wounded Healer" Temptation
People in the helping professions have been the subject of considerable research by psychologists and sociologists, who note that a high percentage of them are "wounded healers" who find healing for their own personal wounds by helping to heal others. For ministers, physicians, nurses, or social workers, the drive to serve others to the detriment of oneself may be partially fueled by inner needs distinct from the passion to serve. Thus, caregivers come full circle: they start as wounded children whose need to heal flows from those wounds, then they become wounded healers as doctors, nurses, or social

workers, and end up as "healers wounded" because they have not taken compassionate care of themselves.

Being a wounded healer is not necessarily a bad thing. Healers can come into being either in spite of or because of their own vulnerabilities and anguish. One can be led to a life of self-denial through personal struggle with suffering. Feeling one is doing all that one must often requires being overworked and exhausted. Faced with suffering patients, a caregiver's own family, interests, or need for rest arouse an unquenchable guilt.

The "Excellence" Temptation

Caregivers, especially physicians, live under another imperative that tempts them to overwork—the imperative to excel. It starts as early as high school, takes hold in the college premed program, and goes into overdrive in medical school. Average students are not accepted into prestigious medical schools or residency programs. Thus the pressure to excel is enormous, and if it is exacerbated by family expectations, it can be overwhelming. One physician admitted to me that he had been driven to perform because his father expected excellence. When he proudly told his father that he had graduated second in his medical school class, his disappointed father had asked, "Why weren't you number one?"

Since no one wants to be just an average caregiver, excellence requires diligence, sacrifice, and single-minded devotion. Breakthrough medical research, superior outcomes in surgery, or superior diagnosis and treatment do not reward those who limit their efforts to 50 or 60 hours a week. Moreover, as in most professions, there has been enormous pressure of late for healthcare providers to increase productivity and performance. Staying on the cutting edge now requires more time than ever.

Once again, the dilemma arises: an emotional or ethical imperative (or both) to do one's best can conflict with the imperative to nurture one's relationships and one's own humanity. The needs of others and the desire for excellence conspire to make physicians ignore their own welfare. Caring for others and pursuing excellence become inimical to the self's need for rest and balance.

The "Denial of Death" Temptation

Psychologists and philosophers have theorized that a passion to serve with excellence may, at a preconscious level, be a way to cope with one's own mortality. Ernest Becker's prize-winning book *The Denial of Death* persuaded me that denying our mortality—not repressing our sexuality, as Freud theorized—breeds most of our anxieties and neuroses. Promiscuity, the hunger for power, wealth, and notoriety, and the drive to work ourselves to exhaustion, Becker insists, are often due to the subconscious terror that haunts us in our finitude.[5]

Morrie Schwartz echoed this sentiment when he told his biographer Mitch Albom, "Well, the truth is, if you really listen to that bird on your shoulder, if you accept that you can die at any time—then you might not be as ambitious as you are."[6] We humans excel at escaping unpleasant realities, not the least of which is the fact that we are going to die, perhaps at any moment. Only when death becomes a very real and imminent prospect do we realize that our attempts at escape are useless. It is then we must discover our true selves and decide whether external qualities such as professional success or failure define the core of who we are. Much of our obsessive activity—even for the noblest ethical reasons—keeps us from facing this reality. As Jerome Miller so eloquently wrote in his essay, "The Way of Suffering":

> To be stricken by grief means precisely to have one's managerial control over one's life . . . incapacitated by it. The therapeutic effort to bring grief into the open to talk about death without our old hesitancies and reluctances, has, I think, the unintended effect of transforming the experience of death so that we can . . . undergo it without being ultimately upset by it. It judges suffering from the point of view of ordinary life and so tries to deprive it of its very capacity to rupture that life irreparably. In that sense, it never sees things from the point of view of the sufferer. For the sufferer may be close to a truth that the therapeutic way of thinking never leads us to suspect—that our whole ordinary way of life, with all its evasions and avoidances, is in some profound sense unreal. Suffering has a way of turning everything upside down. And from that overturned perspective, it makes no sense to resume one's ordinary life— because one knows now the truths it was designed

to keep hidden. In that sense, someone who truly encounters death can never recover, for he cannot resume the way of life that sheltered him from the very intimation of it.[7]

It is no secret that excessive paperwork, patient volume, declining income, and diminishing personal time are a major frustration for caregivers. Physicians and nurses tell me that the primary source of their burnout is the tension between the conflicting expectations of the healthcare system and their patients. HMO's and insurance companies demand efficiency. This puts pressure on physicians to spend less time per patient and to use scarce resources more effectively. Patients, meanwhile, want more attention from doctors and access to any tests and procedures that might prove beneficial.

Caregivers know they have chosen a demanding, stressful profession filled with beepers, early morning calls, and a time-consuming, paper-filled reimbursement mechanism. They don't like the present system, but are not sure what a better alternative would look like. So they cope as best they can, and we should be thankful they do. "It's not the money," one young physician, who was barely making enough as a primary care physician to support his family, told me. "If I had wanted money, I would have gotten an MBA, not an MD."

§

God's Answer to Burnout

So what is to be done? Perhaps the idea of sabbath, a theme running throughout Scripture, can lead us to a solution.

In March of 2006, like many men my age, I was diagnosed with prostate cancer. The following August, after considerable discussion with other prostate cancer patients, radiation oncologists, and surgeons, I decided to undergo a laparoscopic radical prostatectomy at the Lahey Clinic just outside Boston, near the cottage in Maine's Belgrade Lakes where my wife and I often spend the summer. The surgery began at 7 a.m. on August 16, my wedding anniversary. While I spent much of the next day in and out of sleep, sometime in the early hours I awoke and called the nurse. "I want to get up and walk," I said, and hanging on to her and my I.V. pole I did—for about 15 minutes.

By noon the next day I was reasonably alert and ready to leave the hospital. My postoperative instructions included an interesting regimen: For the first week or so I was to rest for 40 minutes of every hour and walk (very gingerly at first) for the remaining 20 minutes. "You must walk," I was told, "but not for more than 20 minutes at a time for at least the first couple of weeks." Walk, rest, walk, rest. It reminded me of the natural cycle that supports all living things. Plants have cycles of growth and dormancy; even the land in which plants grow rests every winter. Animals and human beings experience their own daily cycles. Activity and work deplete energy and strength; rest and sleep restore—even enhance—them. The walk and rest cycles of my recovery were as necessary for my cure from cancer as was my surgery.

Just recently I underwent yet another surgery, this time for a hernia. My urologist told me that many men do not rest enough before resuming normal activity after such a procedure. Three weeks after surgery they feel great again and want to start running and lifting weights, but the body needs at least three more weeks to enjoy a complete cure. In other words, one must rest beyond the point of feeling rested. A sprained ankle needs time to heal before it is ready to bear the body's weight, even if the pain is tolerable. Rest, then, is essential to curing our ailments and, as we shall see, healing our relationships.

As we get older, more rest and sleep is required to maintain our declining strength. I am amazed at the ability of my 15-year-old grandson and 12-year-old granddaughter to endure "sleepovers" (a misnomer, to be sure, as they almost always involve significant loss of sleep) with their friends and still jump into the next day's activities with high energy. Of course, it catches up with them eventually but, speaking for myself, staying up half the night with my friends is about as appealing as a root canal.

Restoring or maintaining health through the cycle of work and rest is woven into the world's tapestry. It is also woven into Scripture. In Genesis we find that it all began at the creation sabbath, when rest was invested with a divine dimension. Christians who fail to grasp the importance of a sabbath rest are impoverished and vulnerable when misfortune fires its salvos of disease and sickness. They realize then that what they thought was merely a day set aside for worship and fellowship is also—seen through contemporary lenses—a time for curing and healing.

The story of the sabbath begins with the announcement that on the seventh day of creation God rested from his efforts of forming the earth and its inhabitants:

> Thus the heavens and the earth were finished, and all their multitude. And on the seventh day God finished the work that he had done, and he rested on the seventh day from all the work that he had done. So God blessed the seventh day and hallowed it, because on it God rested from all the work that he had done in creation (Genesis 2:1-3).

Understandably, Jewish and Christian theologians have wondered what to make of the idea of God "resting" from anything. Obviously, it cannot mean that God suffered from muscular fatigue the way we do. Most have concluded that it signifies that in God's universe, ceaseless activity is not the ideal. The active life must be punctuated with rest that revels in the wonders of creation and human community.

Genesis says that when God finished the creation he saw that it was "good"; therefore, God rested on the seventh day and pronounced it "holy." The sabbath symbolizes God's satisfaction and joy at the completion of his remarkable work—the creation of the Earth and its varied and fecund life forms, and the freedom bestowed on human beings, the only creatures made in God's image. One gets the feeling from the text that at this stage the world was perfect in design and harmony. The long shadows of sin, suffering, and death to come could not diminish the light of divine life that infused everything.

Little or nothing more is said about the sabbath until the book of Exodus, named for a divine liberation so dramatic it still inspires quests for freedom, from the Civil Rights movement in America to the struggle against apartheid in South Africa. As Exodus tells it, from sunup to sundown, seven days a week for centuries, Hebrews slaved in unspeakable cruelty under Egyptian pharaohs. It is astonishing to think about: not one day of worship or rest for generations! No wonder the Hebrews cried for deliverance. God "heard their cries," the Bible says, and intervened, using Moses to deliver the slaves in a spectacular fashion. When liberation from Egypt was complete, Moses went up into Mt. Sinai to receive God's laws, expressed as the Ten Commandments and understood to be the core of Hebrew identity. Virtually in the middle of that core was this commandment:

> Remember the sabbath day, and keep it holy. Six days you shall labor and do all your work. But the seventh day is a sabbath to the Lord your God; you shall not do any work—you, your son or your daughter, your male or female slave, your livestock, or the alien resident in your towns. For in six days the Lord made heaven and earth, the sea, and all that is in them, but rested the seventh

day; therefore the Lord blessed the sabbath day and consecrated it (Exodus 20:8-11).

Imagine the impact of these words. A people enslaved for centuries were now *commanded* to rest every seven days, as God had rested at creation. An exhausted race was instructed to rest and enjoy the created world and the human beings in it. As if to emphasize this connection, the sabbath commandment reported in Deuteronomy does not ground the sabbath rest in creation, but in the Hebrew Exodus itself:

> Observe the sabbath day and keep it holy, as the Lord your God commanded you. Six days you shall labor and do all your work. But the seventh day is a sabbath to the Lord our God; you shall not do any work—you, or your son or daughter, or your male or female slave, or your ox or your donkey, or any of your livestock, or the resident alien in your towns, so that your male and female slave may rest as well as you. *Remember that you were a slave in the land of Egypt, and the Lord your God brought you out with a mighty hand and an outstretched arm; therefore the Lord your God commanded you to keep the sabbath day* (Deuteronomy 5:12-15, emphasis mine).

Unlike the Exodus commandment, which focused on God's power to create, Deuteronomy celebrates God's activity *in* creation itself as the redeemer from Egyptian slavery. When these slave laborers were told that they were to rest out of gratitude to Yahweh, they understood that labor must never be an end in itself, not even labor for good things.

Since God has acted on our behalf, we too are commanded to rest. The fact of what God has done for us undergirds the requirement to obey God by resting ourselves and enjoining all others over whom we have authority to rest as well. The powerless cannot be forced to work unremittingly without disobeying God. What freedom to go from being forced to work to being commanded to rest! Without periodic rest from labor, human life cannot flourish. Under the pressure of unrelenting stress, such as that imposed on the Hebrew slaves, we now know that the human immune system becomes depleted. Life, as Thomas Hobbes so aptly phrased it, becomes "nasty, brutish, and short." In our own era, we have witnessed the horrendous effects of slave labor camps in the Soviet Union and Nazi Germany. Offered little or no food and minimal protection from the elements, a shocking percentage of laborers perished long before their time. In his groundbreaking book on concentration camp survivors, *Man's Search for Meaning*,[8] psychiatrist Viktor Frankl argued that even in these direst of conditions, men and women, in the rare moments when they were given time to reflect and rest, continually searched for meaning.

Once liberated from the camps, the few who survived experienced rest as a cure, even a reversal of their stress-related ailments, for while stress debilitates the immune system, rest empowers it. An empowered immune system prevents innumerable diseases and ailments. Even today, we need to be reminded that rest is as important to physical and emotional health as is work, food, and protection from the elements. Doctors today bemoan the way American culture has devalued rest. While we are not literally enslaved, our freedom is curtailed by 60-to 80-hour work weeks, the ceaseless interruptions of communications technology, and a narcissistic need to "succeed" (whatever that means) at all costs. "Worked himself into an early grave" was a frequent epitaph during the Industrial Revolution when long, arduous hours in coal mines and manufacturing plants literally killed people a little each day. If we are not careful, it could be said of us today.

§

Curing and Healing Through Rest

We saw in chapter 1 that during the time of Jesus curing sickness was inseparable from healing people's broken relationships with God and with their kin. Sickness and disease were assumed to be divine punishments for personal or family sins. In the act of curing human disease, Jesus also healed the sufferers, for now they were no longer seen as offending God and polluting society. They were healed and forgiven at the same time.

The sabbath rest is imbued with this multilayered concept of curing and healing through forgiveness. The command to rest implies much more than a cessation of physical labor. The Hebrews were to give time to God in worship, to their families in hours of refreshing conversation and recreative activity, and to their community in fellowship and service. For us today, observing the sabbath rest means attending to the needs of imperfect relationships with God and with each other. This day reminds us that our most significant achievements are not in the world of commerce but in the intimacies we enjoy with God, family, and our worshipping community. These interactions heal us in so many ways and at so many levels, it is impossible to adequately chronicle them.

In 2008, renowned journalist Tim Russert of NBC's "Meet the Press" and Tony Snow, former press secretary to President George W. Bush, both passed away. Russert's death from cardiac failure was sudden and unexpected, while Snow had battled cancer for years. In both cases, while news stories rightly recounted both men's outstanding professional achievements, much more time and space was given to their devotion to their families. In Russert's case, his passion for the Roman Catholic Church was also mentioned again and again. In the days before his death he had gone to Italy with his family to celebrate his son's graduation from Boston College. The outpouring of affection and respect that these men received is evidence that our greatest admiration is for people who work very hard and achieve great things and take the time to nurture a loving and satisfying family life. At life's end, we honor the professionally successful, but we envy those whose families were nourished by their devotion.

Some years ago I was invited to preach to an African-American congregation in the Roxbury neighborhood of Boston. Knowing the practices of this church, I asked the pastor how it was that black worshippers tolerate much longer church services than white congregations do, often staying for services that last all day. His thoughtful response moved me deeply. "Jim," he said, "you have to remember that all week long most of my members work in low-paying jobs and endure racism that demeans and diminishes them. Their lives are filled with struggle. On the sabbath, they come to church to rest from those struggles and get refreshed to face the week ahead. They don't 'tolerate' church services, they eat them up! It takes all day to get them ready to face another week." Quality time with their families, exciting worship services filled with joyous singing and interactive preaching, and nurturing their deepest friendships—all happening at once—brew an elixir they must drink in every week.

The importance of quality time for quality relationships comes into sharp focus in times of suffering and sickness. People who need healing (especially when they cannot be cured) worry more about those they love than about themselves. My father-in-law told me that he endured the nightmare of chemotherapy for his metastasized cancer in order to give his wife one more year of his time. Those who know their time on earth is limited crave spending what remains enjoying the most powerful relationships in their lives. In the final analysis, knowing they are loved and loving in return is what gives their final hours meaning.

A film I saw recently reminded me of this deep need. "How About You" chronicles the lives of a group of quirky, bitter, self-absorbed people in a retirement community who won't even deign to eat with each other at mealtimes. The lead male character is a retired, alcoholic judge who deeply regrets not keeping the promise he made to his wife to sober up before she died. Now sober, he is nonetheless unpleasant, insulting, demanding, and arrogant to everyone. Another resident is a retired dancer who pines for her youth when life was filled with fun. Still another is a woman whose father forced her to give up her only son for adoption, then locked her in a closet for months as punishment. She had wanted to marry the father—an artist—and was prevented from doing so. Her own artistic gifts were suppressed, and now she keeps to herself, refusing to go out, not allowing anyone into her small apartment filled with drawings and paintings of people in the retirement community and from her past.

This acrimonious pot is stirred by a young, irreverent woman who comes to work at the home. Her sister, the owner, has had difficulty retaining help because of the residents' antisocial behavior. When the owner leaves for a few weeks to care for an elderly relative, the young woman is left free to do more or less as she pleases, which alternates between connecting with them in new, creative ways and confronting them over their ridiculous conduct. In the end, healing occurs as openness, vulnerability, and honesty triumph over self-protection and bickering. Fun returns and they begin— haltingly—to eat with each other in the dining room, go out together to a local pub, and create a magnificent Christmas feast. This was a story about healing of the kind so many families and communities need.

JAMES J. LONDIS

§

Caregiver Rest and a Clear Conscience

Oddly enough, many of the people who most need the healing embedded in sabbath time are the nurses, physicians, and other caregivers who work to cure others of their physical ailments. Can these caregivers, especially those who are people of faith, achieve a balance between work and rest without feeling the remorse inherent in Jesus' admonition, "This you ought to have done, and not left the other undone" (Matt. 23:23)? I have seen this dilemma plague countless hospital physicians and residents, especially those who are also young parents.[9] The solution lies in a shift in our cultural values. As a Christian, I have been surprised and gratified by the number of contemporary writers who urge a return to the notion of a weekly sabbath as a remedy for overly busy and stressed people who seek to love others as Jesus did. As one of these writers put it:

> God graces us with rest, and, as we respond with
> our gratitude, receiving the gift, we begin to enter
> into that balanced life which is our destiny as the
> people of a loving creator.[10]

If caregivers deny themselves adequate rest because they believe that is what God requires of them as disciples of the "Great Physician," they need to recall that God's initial word on the sabbath was not an invitation to rest. An invitation would not adequately address the problem. They need to recognize that the sabbath commandment is just that—a commandment that locates the imperative to rest within divinity itself; that is, if God rested as the Creator, we who are made in God's image must also rest. Note that this rest is not merely a cessation of activity, but an intentional rest that alters how we spend our time in ordinary living. It is to be a rest so extraordinary that it teaches us the meaning and significance of ordinary time and labor. All creation—including animals, slaves, foreigners, and the land itself—is to be recreated and renewed by this rest. Refusing to rest is not an option, but is tantamount to idolizing labor and defacing God's image in the creation. Furthermore, this obligatory rest should not be seen as a burden (though many believers act as if it were). As a Jewish rabbi once said, "The sabbath is a burden in the same way that pushing a wheelbarrow full of diamonds is a burden."

The writer of the New Testament epistle to the Hebrews connects the sabbath to the new covenant in Christ by using it as a symbol of the rest that awaits God's people at the end of history (Heb. 4:1-6). The creator will recreate the world, the liberator from slavery will liberate the cosmos from evil, and we shall all rest from the fear of suffering and death. If we look forward to our ultimate rest in God, how can we not grasp the importance of rest for the present?

For these reasons, physicians and other caregivers may not justify or indulge in overwork, even when their compassion drives them to it. Nor can they defend self-destructive overwork because they have heard the "call of God" to heal the sick and wounded. The sabbath commandment clearly means that caregivers' obligations to their patients must be subordinate to the divine imperative to rest. In other words, for believers, religious commitments must take priority over ethical commitments. Caregivers must resist the kind of hubris that makes them believe they are indispensable, for the sabbath commandment reminds them that no matter how hard they work, they will not cure all disease or relieve all suffering. To work as if they are trying to assume this responsibility denies their creatureliness and tempts them to stand in the place of God.

In this way, the sabbath commandment prohibits turning service to others into an idol. It is as if God is saying, "It is good that you have passionately participated in the work of my kingdom by seeking to heal the wounded, weak, and vulnerable. But it is my responsibility—not yours—to make an ultimate difference. In the fullness of time, I will cure all disease, relieve all suffering, and ensure eternal life for your dying patients." The sabbath orders us to interrupt the daily grind that depletes us. Like Mother Theresa's daily prayers, Thomas Merton's contemplative retreats, or Billy Graham's reading of a Psalm every morning, this time of rest is to be inviolate. It is meant to be a corrective to our tendency to work much too hard for noble reasons, and because God demands it, we don't need to feel selfish if we say no to the needs of others in order to embrace this time.

You may say, "This is all very well for believers who worship within a sabbath tradition, but what about those who are not religious? How can the sabbath help them?" It seems to me that, with or without a divine rationale, the same considerations are valid. Everything we know about nature and life suggests the importance of a cycle of work and rest, a secular parallel to the sabbath. One contemporary witness to this insight is the poet and writer Kathleen Norris, who, while an agnostic, nonetheless entered a monastery for a season of rest and reflection. It was as though her life itself were telling her she needed a sabbath.

The sabbath urges us to admit our finitude and, if we believe in God, to trust him. We must remember that he has only called us to respond to our neighbors in the manner of the Good Samaritan, not to heal all the evils of the world.

The sabbath also addresses the wounded healer's susceptibility to overwork and burnout. The wounded healer may become the "healer wounded," a caregiver whose need to be healed through service becomes pathological. Through the gift of sabbath rest, God can transform our most painful childhood experiences into strengths that can be used in the service of others. Our vulnerability can be transformed into sensitivity to our patients and others who are hurting.

Sabbath rest also addresses the danger of idolizing excellence. Healthcare demands academic and technical excellence. Human life is on the line—no trivial matter. But I believe the sabbath redefines excellence by making it more inclusive. That is, excellence in human existence as a whole must be the goal. One-dimensional, overworked people cannot serve God or the ill faithfully. One could argue that working seven days a week from sunup to sundown made the Hebrews the finest slaves ever conscripted and the weakest community ever called to be a nation. Rollo May observed in his book *The Courage to Create* that creative people do their best work while walking on the beach or shaving in the morning, not while toiling over their tasks. Relaxation, with the mind focused on other things, offers the creative breakthroughs we seek. I find that my best ideas come after I have been sleeping for several hours. When I wake up, the things I have been thinking about with some confusion fall into place and I have to get up and write them down.

What about our battle with our sense of mortality? Can the sabbath provide relief here? Working excessively hard on behalf of others can confer a sense of historical importance. We all want our influence and memory to continue beyond our deaths. But sabbath rest reminds us that there is only one adequate solution to the specter of death: the reality of a God whose power is greater than the grave. There is no more immortality by works in the Christian faith than there is righteousness by works; it is the gift of God.

Believing caregivers may have their own objections to this proposal. Students of the Scriptures know that the one very clear exception to the sabbath commandment is Jesus' teaching that one cannot refuse to heal or save life on the sabbath. We are not only free to "lift the ox out of the pit," but we are enjoined to do so. It is an obligation that stands in tension with the obligation to sabbath rest. Luke tells the story of a man whose right hand was withered who came to the synagogue on the sabbath (Luke 6:6-11). The Pharisees "watched [Jesus] to see whether he would cure on the sabbath, so that they might find an accusation against him" (v. 8). Jesus could easily have waited until sundown to heal the man, but he challenged his onlookers: "'I ask you, is it lawful to do good or to do harm on the sabbath, to save life or destroy it?" No one responded, so Jesus ordered the man to stretch out his hand, and his hand was "restored."

On its surface, this episode might seem to re-impose the caregiver's burden. How can an exhausted caregiver refuse healing to someone in order to take a rest? To answer, we must go back to the commandment itself as given in both Exodus and Deuteronomy: All must rest. I believe that includes caregivers. It is a given that any physician, nurse, therapist, or technician on any sabbath may be morally and religiously required to work to heal and save life. What is not a given is that every caregiver on every sabbath is required to do so. And should the caregiver have to work on a particular sabbath, the caregiver must be mindful that healing on the day of rest is itself an act of worship to God that fulfills the purpose of the day. It is holy labor, equivalent to the labor of ministers or priests. That kind of labor is within the sabbath rest rather than an exception to it. Entered into properly, it is another way of resting. However, a cautionary note: Our motives are notoriously self-deceiving. We must valiantly examine ourselves to be sure we are not working on the sabbath for profits rather than patients.

Because God's eternity enfolds us in our Sabbath celebrations . . . we will delight in becoming agents for [God's] purpose of caring for the poor, delivering the oppressed, announcing the good news of salvation, building peace in the world— not with any false idealism that we can bring the kingdom of God to its culmination in the world, but with the sure hope that God is always at work to create peace and justice and freedom and that we can participate in his eternal purpose because of the Holy Spirit's power within us.[11]

Healthcare professionals called to healing for ethical and religious reasons are easy targets for excessive, self-destructive self-denial. The invitation and command to keep the sabbath rest is designed, in part, to provide balance for them and to assure them that, even when they rest, God continues to work for their patients in ways that are full of wonder. It also imposes on the faith-based healthcare community the responsibility to design systems, policies, and procedures that provide adequate rest for caregivers, so that they may be healed even as they are healing. There may be no better way to truly witness to our religious heritage of medical ministry than to have faith that the Great Physician will, through us, do everything possible for our patients, even as we enter into the rest God designed for us to enjoy.

Notes and References

[1]Palmer, Parker J. *The Active Life: A Spirituality of Work, Creativity and Caring* (New York: Harper & Row, 1990), pp. 9-11; quoted in Don Postema, *Catch Your Breath: God's Invitation to Sabbath Rest* (Grand Rapids, CRC Publications, 1997), p. 45.

[2]Remen, Rachel Naomi. *Kitchen Table Wisdom: Stories That Heal* (New York: Riverhead Books, 1994).

[3]Steele, Richard B. "Unremitting Compassion: The Moral Psychology of Parenting Children with Genetic Disorders." *Theology Today* (June 2000), 162.

[4]Steele, 164.

[5]Becker, Ernest. *The Denial of Death* (New York: The Free Press , 1973).

[6]Albom, Mitch. *Tuesdays With Morrie* (New York: Doubleday, 1997), 81.

[7]Jerome A. Miller's unpublished essay entitled "The Way of Suffering" won an award at the Colloquium of the Basic Issues Forum, held October 17-18, 1986 at Washington and Jefferson College in Washington, PA.

[8]Frankl, Viktor E. *Man's Search for Meaning* (Boston: Beacon Press, 2006; first published in 1946).

[9]Because so many women are now entering the field of medicine (and a good thing, too, or we would have an incredible shortage of physicians), it is important to add that studies on physician burnout have identified gender as a significant issue. The June 1, 2000 *Journal of General Internal Medicine* (Vol. 15, Issue 6, pp. 372-380) reported that female physicians were more likely to report satisfaction with their specialty and with patient and colleague relationships, but less likely to be satisfied with autonomy, relationships with the community, pay, and resources. Compared to their male colleagues, female physicians also reported treating the same number of patients overall, but more female patients and more patients with complex psychosocial problems. Time pressure in ambulatory settings was greater for women, who on average reported needing 36% more time than allotted to provide quality care for new patients or consultations, compared with 21% more time needed by men. When controlling for multiple factors, mean income for women was approximately $22,000 less than that of men. Women were 1.6 times more likely to report burnout than men, with the odds of burnout by women increasing by 12% to 15% for each additional 5 hours over 40 worked per week. Lack of workplace control predicted burnout in women, but not in men. For female physicians with young children, odds of burnout were 40% less when support was received from colleagues, spouse, or significant other to balance work and home issues.

[10]Canahan, Elizabeth J. "A Rest Remaining." Quoted in: Postema, Don. *Catch Your Breath: God's Invitation to Sabbath Rest* (Grand Rapids, MI: CRC Publications, 1997).

[11]Dawn, Marva J. *Keeping the Sabbath Wholly: Ceasing, Resting, Embracing, Feasting* (Grand Rapids, MI: Eerdmans, 1989), 104-105.

Issue Four

༄

Suffering, Prayer, and God's Plan for Our Lives

Questions from Suffering

When faced with suffering or tragedy—the untimely death of a spouse or child, crippling or disfigurement from a freak accident, the onset of progressive disease, the nightmare of a natural disaster, it makes little difference—most of us ask the same question: "Why did this happen to me?" Christians usually put an extra spin on this question, asking, "Why did God send or allow this to happen to me?" That question embodies an ancient and ongoing argument about God's role in evil and the suffering it brings in its wake.

Convinced that God could and should have prevented their anguish, I have heard Christians curse God in their frustration, resolutely challenging the Creator to account for himself: "Are you in control or not? Is this suffering in your plan for my life? What kind of God allows such things to happen to those who love and serve him? Don't your promises to protect your children mean anything? Or are you just turning up the heat to 'refine' us with fire? Is this your way of strengthening our faith and purifying us? How are we supposed to pray when we feel like the targets of your wrath or neglect?"

These questions are voiced in the Book of Psalms, perhaps the most devotional book in Scripture. Many of the psalms, which are actually songs, express Israel's suffering as a nation: "O Lord God of hosts, how long will you be angry with your people's prayers? You have fed them with the bread of tears, and given them tears to drink in full measure" (Psalm 80:4-5). Others utter the cry of an individual: "My God, my God, why have you forsaken me? Why are you so far from helping me, from the words of my groaning? O my God, I cry by day, but you do not answer; and by night, but find no rest" (Psalm 22:1-2).

At the heart of these anguished cries and questions is the assumption of a causal relationship between the goodness or wickedness of our actions and what subsequently happens to us. Many believers are uncomfortable with the notion that God may not exercise absolute control over the events of our lives or the world at large, or that he may not be doling out judgment on a daily basis. It doesn't fit their worldview to think that some things might happen at random or as a natural consequence of a series of human actions. Thus, biblical promises of protection, given to comfort believers, are often misinterpreted: "God is our refuge and strength, a very present help in trouble. Therefore we will not fear, though the mountains shake in the heart of the sea; though its waters roar and foam, though the mountains tremble with its tumult" (Psalm 46:1-3). "A thousand shall fall at your side and ten thousand at your right hand, but it will not come near you" (Psalm 91:7). "It will not come near you" strikes these believers as a guarantee that they will be shielded from the consequences of natural or political upheavals. When this turns out not to be the case, their anguish is intensified.

To comfort them, many pastors urge their parishioners to trust God implicitly even when their "whys" yield no satisfactory answers. "God's ways are mysterious," the pastors say, and like Job, "we must trust God even if God slays us." But is this the best we can offer to suffering believers who cry, "I prayed every day for the safety of my child, and yet she is gone," or "I followed the biblical counsel to have the church elders pray for me during my illness, but nothing happened"? At times like these, people want more than reassuring words; they want to know why God is absent, seemingly silent and unresponsive to their needs.

I find that appeals to God's inscrutability do not help suffering patients and their families very much. Nor do statements that suggest God is trying to teach or perfect the believer through suffering. A believer's torment in the face of God's seeming unresponsiveness raises unavoidable questions about God's role in our personal lives, in world events that affect our lives, and in our ability to understand and achieve God's purposes for us. Is a child's death part of God's plan? Was the 2004 Indian Ocean tsunami punishment for the sins of the Indonesian people as some Imams suggested? Is there really a reason why, as Rabbi Harold Kushner asked in his bestselling book,[1] "bad things happen to good people"? Can God ignore the cries of His children and still be a loving God?

§

God's Plan and Our Suffering

Christian preachers who declare that God has a specific plan and purpose for each life are amazingly popular in contemporary culture. They teach that unless believers discern God's intended purpose for their lives, they will never find true joy. Those who hear this message can become quite perplexed. When their preacher says, "God has a plan for you," he may simply be saying that God knows the future and their place in it, and that the "plan" is merely the future that God sees. Or he may be saying that God devises the future they are to have and organizes their life events to bring about that future. To many, this suggests that God has "planned" that they should suffer, and that when disaster strikes they should pray for discernment to see how their suffering fits into God's plan for their lives.

Preachers of this message often quote the prophet Jeremiah to buttress their argument that God has a plan for each of us even before we are born:

> Now the word of the Lord came to me saying, "Before I formed you in the womb I knew you, and before you were born I consecrated you; I appointed you a prophet to the nations" (Jeremiah 1:4-5).

It is difficult to decipher the exact meaning of this passage. Taken literally, it is easy to conclude that God has a detailed plan for our lives that begins before we are conceived, and that we ignore that plan at our peril. The phrase "before I formed you" suggests that God personally and actively created the fetus that would be born as Jeremiah. This is incomprehensible to modern readers, given our knowledge of the biology of procreation.

The passage focuses on the divine element in our lives and pays no attention whatsoever to the human factor. But to think soundly and reasonably about this issue, we must pay attention to the human factor. For example, it is acutely difficult to understand how this passage relates to human beings conceived by rape or incest or outside of a committed relationship, as so often happens to teenagers. Traditional Christian preachers can say that God "knew" this child would be conceived, but how can they say that God *planned* or *intended* that anyone should be born through a process that violates the divine will? How could God plan that a pregnancy result from rape, incest, or immature judgment accomplish his divine purpose without justifying those criminal or evil actions, and even being partly responsible for them? Personally, I believe that saying these events were specifically planned or allowed by God to accomplish his purposes is a cruel attempt to turn a tragedy into a triumph.

I also find this understanding of God's role in our lives, including our suffering, impossible to reconcile with either the teachings of Jesus or my own life story. It is one thing to assert that God knew I would be born and planned accordingly (though many doubt even that, as we shall see). It is quite another to say my birth was in his eternal plan in the sense that my existence *had* to be, irrespective of human choice, suggesting that God set events in motion to come out a certain way.

As far as I can tell, my parents did not plan to have me when they were first married, but birth control methods back then were primitive at best. My arrival meant that my 23-year-old father, who worked in a low-paying job, lost the earning power of my 18-year-old mother. This put our family on—if not over—the edge of real poverty. I also doubt very much that they planned to have my brother 14 months later, an arrival that only exacerbated our problems. My parents separated when I was a child, driving my mother and her by then three boys even deeper into indigence. We survived on welfare, charity, and sporadic financial support from my maternal grandmother, as well as the occasional check from my father who was trying to get an education and build a new life for himself. Yet some would have me believe that God planned that I be born to poor, unprepared parents and raised by a young, overwhelmed mother; that what my parents never planned *was* in God's plan, and that the events of my childhood were purposed by God to make me what I am today.

I teach at Kettering College of Medical Arts in Kettering, Ohio. In January 2007 a colleague of mine was crossing Southern Boulevard in front of the school, as she had hundreds of times before. As she was standing in the pedestrian median waiting for traffic to clear, a distraught driver following the ambulance carrying her mother to the nearby hospital struck my friend a glancing blow, resulting in numerous broken bones and multiple surgeries. Who planned that this should happen? Certainly not my injured friend, nor the driver fearful for her mother's life. But again, some would insist it was part of God's plan.

The news media are full of countless other incidents that make us question God's hand in human events. In late 2006, three experienced climbers undertook a winter ascent of Oregon's Mt. Hood, as they had done many times before. Kelly James said he loved to climb because nothing else brought him so close to God. But that year, an unexpected blizzard and James's shoulder injury initiated a series of events that caused him and his fellow climbers to perish. No one would say that was their plan, but many would argue that it was God's plan.

We plan to have happy marriages, yet end up in bitter divorces. We pray for and plan for healthy children, yet every year thousands of parents give birth to babies whose disabilities create a lifelong burden. We plan lovely vacations climbing a mountain or relaxing on a beach in Indonesia, only to find ourselves in the path of a horrendous natural disaster. Whose plan is this?

§

Freedom—Within Limits

Life does not always go according to our plan because we have considerable, but not absolute, power over what happens to us. We can choose to work at Kettering College and decide to cross Southern Boulevard at a certain time, but we cannot control the moment a frightened driver passes too close to us. We can control when we ascend Mt. Hood, but not when a blizzard descends on it. When our limited control confronts the random uncertainty of life, many Christians cling to the belief that God controls everything that happens to them, that things always go according to God's plan because God plans all things. It's as if the biblical story of Job were being replayed again and again in every human life. God decides when, how much, and how long each of us will suffer. This belief comforts many of the faithful, who seem to disregard the fact that in the narrative, Job's sufferings were allowed (not caused) by God for cosmically significant reasons. This distinction between "allowed" and "caused" is not really very helpful for believers if they are going to insist that each event of their lives is part of God's plan. They believe that, as Christ's followers, our task is to discern God's plan not only in every decision we make (what school we attend, what career we choose, who we marry), but to also see God's plan for us in sickness, suffering, tragedy, and death. That in order to be happy, our lives must unfold in harmony with a God-devised plan that we can know only by interpreting some sort of divine "tea leaves," which indicate how God is leading us to fulfill his ends.

If this is true, it means that God intended that I be born to struggling parents, that my colleague be injured on Southern Boulevard, and that a blizzard on Mt. Hood take the lives of three climbers. Many Christians cling to this belief as if it were a life preserver to keep them from drowning in despair. One of my students declared in class that "if God decided to send me a debilitating illness, he must have a reason and I must try to learn what it is. Nothing happens outside the purposes of God." But theologian David Bentley Hart eloquently states his concerns about such thinking and suggests a better alternative:

> What then, one might well ask, is divine providence? Certainly all Christians must affirm God's transcendent governance of everything, even fallen history and fallen nature, and must believe that by that governance he will defeat evil and bring the final good of all things out of the darkness of "this age." It makes a considerable difference,

however—nothing less than our understanding of the nature of God is at stake—whether one says that God has eternally willed the history of sin and death, and all that comes to pass therein, as the proper or necessary means of achieving his ends, or whether one says instead that God has willed his good in creatures from eternity and will bring it to pass, despite their rebellion, by so ordering all things toward his goodness that even evil (which he does not cause) becomes an occasion of the operations of grace. And it is only the latter view than [sic] can accurately be called a doctrine of "providence" in the properly theological sense; the former view is mere determinism.[2]

I confess that I share Hart's perspective, which indicts the thinking of many conservative Christians and theologians. The idea that God regards sin and death, and their attendant suffering, as essential to accomplishing his purposes is theologically unsound and, in the end, cannot truly comfort believers in their suffering.

Yet, the question remains: Can we at all see God's hand in our daily affairs? Perhaps we can. Alongside the evil and suffering in the world, there is goodness and joy, especially in those moments of love we cherish with our families and friends. Such love can make even chronic illness and death bearable. "God is love" is the cornerstone of the Christian faith and while we can legitimately claim that God's thumbprint is often on deeds of love in the world, not everything we call "love" or "good" should be confused with God. As Jesus warned us, loving one's family can come between us and our love for God.

§

God's Plan and Our Choices

We can and do make poor choices that disrupt our lives and thwart what God knows would be best for us. All believers agree that God's plan for us includes our living virtuously and generously, in faithfulness to the Gospel. Our daily decisions must be made within that overall framework. Respecting our freedom, just as we respect the freedom of our children, God created us to choose for ourselves within the good he wishes for us. That is the creative dimension of being human. We work with God to fashion our lives according to his purposes. To assume that God has decided in advance which college we should attend and who we should marry forces us into trying to determine (through prayer and other means) not how we might make the best possible decision under the guidance of the Holy Spirit, but which of our options God has already chosen for us. I suspect that, like any good parent, God wants to be consulted, wants us to consult other believers and family members who love us, and wants us to think carefully and prayerfully about each decision. But then, I am persuaded, God wants *us* to decide. In that sense we are co-creators, with God, of who and what we will become.

This is not to say that we will never make poor choices. Nor is it to say that we will not make decisions that clearly violate God's will for us. It makes no sense to claim that our bad choices are planned by God. What we *can* say is that our freedom to choose—even to choose badly—is in God's plan. We can also say that while the consequences of our poor choices are not planned by God, living with and being redeemed from those consequences—bad or good—is in God's plan. Paradoxical as it may sound (and this is a case where paradox yields truth), our bad choices are not what God plans, but God's plan takes them into account.

Traditionally, this issue falls under what is known as the doctrine of God's providence and sovereignty. Given the biblical revelation of God as Creator and Redeemer, we are loath to think God is limited or powerless in any circumstance. If God is Lord of all, how can we believe that God relinquishes authority and ultimate control just because we decide wrongly? Can we really sidetrack what God wants for us with our own free will? A biblical example might help.

Absalom was King David's most accomplished and charismatic son. Wildly popular with the people and ambitious to rule without his father, Absalom decided to seize the throne by killing his father. Since Yahweh had established David on the throne, this constituted a rebellion against Yahweh as well. Absalom's plan failed and, in spite of David's command to his troops that Absalom be spared, David's soldiers killed him. So great was David's anguish that it summoned words of grief that haunt readers of the Bible to this day: "O Absalom, my son, my son Absalom; Would I had died instead of you, O Absalom, my son, my son!" (2 Samuel 18:33). While Yahweh clearly intended that David should survive his son's revolt, I do not believe that God intended the revolt to happen in the first place, or necessarily intended that Absalom should die. But these things happened anyway. Both Absalom and David made poor choices. Absalom was vain and arrogant, but David's overindulgence of his son contributed to those qualities. Together, David and Absalom's choices disrupted God's ideal for both of them, but did not ultimately disrupt God's overall plan for Israel. Likewise, our choices can sidetrack God's will for us, but nothing we do can derail God's ultimate plan for his people or his creation. But if we acknowledge that we can choose to disrupt God's plan for us, then we must admit that our freedom requires God to relinquish some control over us and over the events our choices precipitate. God's power over us is therefore self-limited in order that he can wield power for us as we seek to do his will. While God may wield power over us at times, it seems to me it is not to dominate or control but enable us to live the more abundant life. In this way, we become co-creators with God of our destinies.

§

God's Power for Us in Our Suffering

Some Christians refer to their suffering as a "cross" God has given them to bear, and to bear cheerfully. To them, whatever happens, good or bad, *must be* part of God's plan or it could not happen. To support this belief, they often cite the experience of Abraham and Sarah, who were promised that their children would be as numerous as the "sands of the sea." As these believers see it, given Sarah's advanced age, fulfilling this promise would require a "miracle," and in this the biblical writers would have concurred. Their understanding of the biology of procreation was no more advanced than their knowledge of the biological causes of sickness. They believed that pregnancy was a direct result of God's active blessing on a married couple. Conversely, if Sarah could not conceive, it was because God was displeased and had willed that she should not bear children. We all know the sad conclusion of this story. Abraham doubted Yahweh's promise to give him countless descendants through his wife Sarah, so he chose to impregnate Hagar, his servant.

Did God intend that Hagar bear Abraham's child and that she and her son should suffer as a consequence? Not according to the Bible. Hagar's suffering after delivering Ishmael could not have been what God intended without God ceasing to be the God of Jesus Christ. Sarah eventually did conceive as a result of Yahweh's direct intervention, but her case was unique and should not be considered a paradigm for all people in all times and places. Divine involvement in human affairs is not necessarily the same as divine intervention. God strengthening and comforting us throughout our lives (involvement) is not the same as arranging historical events to cause us to conform to a pre-arranged purpose. The vast majority of people who have children conceive them in the manner God established at Creation, without any need for divine intervention. Furthermore, it is clear that God planned that procreation be an option for almost everyone, regardless of their physical, financial, or moral resources, which means that in the natural order of things, children will either benefit or suffer from the circumstances created by their parents. The idea that certain children are intended by God to suffer the consequences of their parents' genetic weaknesses, poverty, or misguided choices amounts to an indictment of the God of love. Parents who choose to drink or become addicted to drugs will likely pass on crippling deficits to their children. Even parents whose behavior is admirable may have children whose needs are overwhelming. Genetics and other well-understood principles *require* that this happen. Yet many believers insist that God's will *overrides* these facts of human existence.

I do not believe that God purposely sends damaged or disabled babies to some parents to refine them through suffering or punish them for their misdeeds. Were God to do that, he would be wielding arbitrary and destructive power over us that would diminish our freedom. By the same token, I do not believe that God wills that certain children be born for the sole purpose of bringing about a specific end—even a blessed one. The November 1, 2007 issue of *USA TODAY* ran a cover story entitled, "An Experiment to Save a Son: Rare Disorder Leads Mother to Desperate Gamble." The story chronicles the battle of the Liao family to save their son Nate, who suffers from a "rare genetic disorder caused by lack of a protein that is needed to keep skin attached to the body. When he rubs his ear, the skin comes off. If someone lifts him from under his arms, his armpits blister. It affects skin inside his body, too. When he throws up, bits of his esophagus come up." Nate's mother, Theresa Liao, would not accept the medical establishment's decision that nothing could be done for Nate. She learned all she could about experimental research on the condition and now there is some small hope for Nate because one of his brothers is a good match for a bone marrow transplant.

Theresa Liao shows astonishing courage as she faces the challenge of saving her son. She believes that someone has to be the first to try the cutting-edge treatment that might save her son's life. "God sent these boys to me for a reason," she muses. "We've made it this far, and worst case, if we have a horrific result, and we have a mortality with Nate, I went down swinging. I'm not only doing this for my kids, but for everybody's kids. I did not do this lightly."

Theresa's conviction that "God sent these boys to me for a reason" is a common sentiment often expressed by parents in dire circumstances. But I do not believe God sent her these particular boys so that the combination of their suffering and her toughness would bring about a cure for this rare disorder. If that were so, God would be wielding power over Theresa in an inappropriate way. I do believe that because this terrible thing happened to her, God will wield power for Theresa by helping her find the strength to do what she is doing for "everybody's kids." God's grace and goodness will always work to bring something meaningful out of human tragedy, but that does not make God responsible for the tragedy.

§

God's Power for Us in Natural Catastrophes

According to the Bible, sin has distorted God's works so that the natural processes set in motion at Creation can sometimes bring suffering and death. The act of procreation gifted to humans can produce healthy babies or sickly ones. In the same way, the natural world that we rely on to sustain us sometimes brings disaster and death to millions. The weather that grows crops also kills thousands each year; the tectonic plates that provide the foundation for all living things can shift under pressure and cause earthquakes and tsunamis. That is the paradox by which life on Earth operates. The fire at the heart of our planet causes volcanic eruptions, but also modulates the atmosphere we depend on for life. The structure of human existence and the operations of the natural world are dependent upon God, but are rarely changed or reoriented by God's direct action, which is why demonstrable miracles are rare and difficult to identify. In an interview published in The Christian Century, Nancey Murphy, philosopher/theologian at Fuller Theological Seminary, put it this way:

> After the tsunami last year I read accounts reflecting on the likely responses to the events by adherents of different faiths. I was startled to see that all of the responses were anthropomorphic— that is, they asked, "Why would God do this to us?" None reflected an appreciation of the fact that plain old natural processes were the cause.[3]

Murphy's interviewer then asked, "Are you saying that we couldn't have the physical order we have in this world without also having the level of disorder we have (assuming the tsunami can be called 'disorder')? Is this another way of saying what the Enlightenment philosophers once maintained— that we live in 'the best of all possible worlds'? Granting that the tsunami was caused by proximate causes, not directly by God, isn't God still somewhere behind the proximate causes?"

Murphy responded, "Yes, geologists can explain why a planet without this recycling of its crust could not support life as we know it. God does not (intentionally) cause tsunamis, but causes there to be a world in which the destruction of life is an unwanted but necessary by-product of the conditions that allow for human life" (*Christian Century*, pp. 47-48). Murphy's comment seems to fly in the face of the biblical promise in Revelation 22 that God intends to create a "new" earth in which the destruction of life will not be necessary to sustain human flourishing. Others might also wonder whether the phrase "causes there to be a world" unnecessarily ignores the doctrine that sin has somehow distorted God's original creation. Nevertheless, God's role in these events is to wield divine power for us by providing comfort and hope for the future, not to wield power over us by manipulating natural events to our advantage.

Philosophy professor and scholar Susan Neiman, director of the Einstein Forum, points out that this urge to see God's hand in every earthly event has a long pedigree. Many 18th-century philosophers had a powerful desire to believe that God was directly responsible for everything that happens. "Suffering that seems entirely random, hence liable to make us doubt God's goodness, would be shown to be the effect of some sin we had secretly committed. Moreover, suffering would be shown to be itself the cause of some greater good, so that the network of causality now partly traceable through the physical universe would be seamlessly extended to the moral one."[4]

§

God-in-Control Thinking and Irresponsibility

A recent article in the *Wall Street Journal*[5] reported on the rift among evangelicals over the issue of global warming. This rift exposes a fundamental disagreement about whether God exercises immediate and direct control over the world. The very meaning of "stewardship" over God's creation is in dispute. One group wants the evangelical political agenda to go beyond abortion and prayer in public schools to include caring for the environment. In Texas, this led to a division among evangelicals over the building of a number of coal-fired power plants. Reverend Frank Brown, pastor of the Bellmead First Baptist Church in the region of the proposed power plant, was not impressed with the eco-evangelicals' concerns. "God," Brown said, "is sovereign over his creation and no amount of coal-burning will alter by a millisecond his divine plan for the world."

While many Christians would dispute Brown's argument, belief in a God who wields absolute control over everything creeps into the daily language of many believers. Some cavalierly add the phrase "God willing" to the end of any statement of plan or intent, meaning it will come to pass if God decides to make it happen. If I say, "I'll see you for breakfast, God willing," and then I am killed on the way to the coffee shop, the suggestion is that God did not will that I should live to meet you. It implies that each event in our lives is a direct consequence of God's immediate activity. That God—in an immediate, not proximate, sense—directly causes everything that happens.

I acknowledge God's sovereignty and that he may intervene at any moment he chooses, but, as I have said, such interventions are rare and difficult to identify. Having worked in healthcare for many years, and having been pastor of a large church for a decade, I can tell you that everyone faced with a dire prognosis prays for a miracle, but very few of those prayers are answered. Acknowledging that there are rare "spontaneous remissions," most disease processes go largely as physicians predict they will. A believer's recovery from cancer may be the result of direct, divine intervention, but many nonbelievers with the same cancers and treatments also recover. One could say that God has given this generation the gift of living in a time when medical cures for some conditions are scientifically possible, making miracles less necessary. Nonetheless, God's role in any specific event is usually enveloped in mystery and not easily discerned, though Christians do not doubt that God's involvement can occur any time he wishes. In my own life, early-stage cancer was discovered by "chance" while I was being tested for another condition. An unusually gifted surgeon and a flawless procedure (guided by God's hands?) resulted in a full recovery. This personal experience, along with those of others, leads me to think it does not seem reasonable to conclude that God intervenes frequently to order everything that happens to us.

§

Suffering as Teaching from God

While running errands recently, I heard a radio preacher tell his congregation that there would be times when God would put them in the "refining fire." They would cry for divine help but none might come. God would let them sit in the "fire" for a while until his purposes for them were accomplished. The preacher quoted Hebrews 12:5-11 to support his view:

> My child, do not regard lightly the discipline of
> the Lord,
> or lose heart when you are punished by him;
> for the Lord disciplines those whom he loves,
> and chastises every child whom he accepts.

> Endure trials for the sake of discipline. God is
> treating you as children; for what child is there
> whom a parent does not discipline? If you do not
> have that discipline in which all children share,

then you are illegitimate and not his children. Moreover, we had human parents to discipline us, and we respected them. Should we not be even more willing to be subject to the Father of spirits and live? For they disciplined us for a short time as seemed best to them, but he disciplines us for our good, in order that we may share his holiness. No, discipline always seems painful rather than pleasant at the time, but later it yields the peaceful fruit of righteousness to those who have been trained by it.

Are we to conclude from these verses, as the radio preacher did, that all painful experiences are part of God's discipline for us? The metaphor in this passage is parenting and the disciplining of children. A central principle of discipline is that it be connected specifically to the behavior or character defect the parent is concerned about. Furthermore, the context of the passage refers to resisting sin as Jesus did. The writer is exhorting us to be faithful witnesses to God's redemptive work in Christ, even when faced with persecution. Suffering for the sake of the Gospel strengthens us in service and disciplines us for challenges not yet faced. We are hardened, in the good sense of the term, against crippling fear as we proclaim God's salvation to the world. This is quite different from arguing that my child's death or my cancer is a discipline from God that I should welcome.

When Jesus called his disciples he warned them that they would face persecution and physical suffering for proclaiming the Gospel. He did not say that any and all suffering they experienced would indicate God's "discipline" of them. When God sends us into darkness to proclaim the light of his truth, there will be a reaction. Suffering for that reason will indeed refine our characters and strengthen us in faithful obedience. We are not being punished to be purified, we are purified because we are punished for Christ's sake. We should not conclude, therefore, that random suffering is sent by God to refine our character.

§

Suffering as Punishment from God

In spite of Jesus' unequivocal statements to the contrary, many people today still choose to believe that God sends them suffering as punishment for youthful sins. While they may realize at some level that many times illness just happens, or that their own lifestyle choices are sufficient explanation for their current physical suffering, they still feel God's punishment in their present circumstance. Christians especially look within when they suffer. "God can do nothing wrong; therefore *I* must have done something wrong for this awful thing to strike me. What have I done that such drastic divine correction has visited me?" This kind of thinking is akin to a pattern psychologists describe in abused children. Children who suffer at the hands of their parents will almost always assume that they brought the abuse upon themselves through their own failings, rather than face the terrifying truth that their parents are fundamentally flawed. I suspect that, in a similar way, it is easier to think that God sends us suffering because we somehow deserve it, than to think that because God has chosen not to exercise absolute control over our lives, we are therefore at the mercy of a random universe.

Some Christians extend this perspective beyond the personal level to global events. God is not only the God of love but the God of judgment, they reason, and God will judge people and even nations for their sins not only in the future but in the here and now. An article in the December 2006 issue of HARPER'S Magazine refers to Christian "historians" who argue that everything that has happened or is happening in American history is part of God's providential plan for this nation. God founded America[6] and protects it from harm. However, when the nation needs to be disciplined, God arranges for that as well. One pastor quoted in the article put it this way:

> God always gave us a left hook of judgment, then He gave us the right cross of revival. . . But when the left hook of the Great Depression came . . . Americans turned to government as their savior instead of God, so we got another left hook, Kennedy's assassination . . . Then another left hook, Vietnam. Still we didn't learn. So God kept throwing punches . . . crack, AIDS, global warming, September 11, 2,500 flag-draped coffins shipped home from Iraq, and more on the way.[7]

If this is true, then God used Lee Harvey Oswald, Osama bin Laden, and Saddam Hussein to punish America. Echoing this sentiment in 2005, Jerry Falwell and Pat Robertson, two leading voices of the Christian right, publicly declared that Hurricane Katrina was God's judgment on the "wicked" city of New Orleans. Others have said that our laws on abortion have brought this nation under the judgment of God, arguing, in effect, that God abandons those who abandon him—a notion flatly contradicted by the teachings of Jesus.

This perspective strikes me as a modern counterpart of the Old Testament writers' conviction that God used nations like Assyria and Babylon to punish Israel for its waywardness and apostasy. But America is not God's "chosen" as Israel was, nor do we live under a theocracy wherein God imposes direct rule over national affairs. Yet somehow this distorted view persists, even though it tends toward blasphemy. As Neiman writes in a discussion of Immanuel Kant, "[he] thought [Enlightenment philosophers] could not possibly believe in the connections between natural and moral evils they asserted without evidence. The claim that all suffering is just payment for some crime or another is belied by ordinary experience every day" (Neiman, p. 69). In other words, nature is indifferent to our purposes and behavior.

As I explained earlier, God's acts (and they are variously interpreted, let me assure you) in the time of ancient Israel should not be taken as a paradigm for how God acts in the present on either a national or global level. From a biblical perspective, God acted directly in the affairs of ancient Israel (as well as in the life and ministry of Jesus) because the plan of salvation required it. Abraham and Sarah's son, according to the narrative, would not have been born without God's intervention. The Exodus happened because God's purposes in the world and in history were at stake. We assume too much if we think the same is true for other nations in other periods which, apparently, are not as essential to achieving God's ultimate purposes for the world.

§

Guidance, Not Control, from God

It would be better if we thought of God's relation to us personally, nationally, or globally as guidance, not control. I am now a satisfied owner of a global positioning system (GPS) device for my automobile and can hardly believe that I waited so long to allow its guidance to come into my life. (I confess to being the typical man who does not like to ask directions, though I have improved as I have gotten older.) This computerized device provides not only maps, but audio directions—in the voice of a woman, no less. Those of you who use them know what I mean. You enter your ultimate destination into the GPS and it automatically determines your current location, tells you how far you have to go, and begins directing you turn by turn and road by road. It warns you well in advance that a turn is coming, then tells you to turn at precisely the right moment. What interests me most about the GPS is what it does when you make a wrong turn or leave the highway to buy gasoline or take a break—it gives you *new directions* to get you back on the right road to your ultimate destination. And it never stops! If you stay off the highway for 100 miles, it will tell you how to get back to it from wherever you are. And if you insist on taking back roads, it will reconfigure the route to your destination and guide you there anyway.

Your decision to either change your destination or make a detour on the way does not frustrate the GPS; it simply offers new guidance. You cannot neutralize the device's power to get you where you need to go. Your choices are yours, but the device is set up to take into account any and all of those choices—good or bad—and keep you moving in the right direction. The "sovereignty" of the GPS cannot be compromised by your refusal to do what it tells you to do. While metaphors should not be stretched too far, the point of this one is rather simple: God's plan for us when we make poor choices is to give us every possible opportunity to learn from those choices and to make a new beginning on our journey. Human life—especially for believers—is structured by God to take into account the mistakes we make that may not only harm but destroy us. To put it another way: *Not everything we as individuals or a nation choose is consistent with God's will, which is always that we choose the best. Yet when we choose poorly, nothing will stop God from helping us recover and move towards living the life of a faithful disciple.* I can decide to ignore my GPS device, but that doesn't change the fact that there is a good and a not-so-good way to get to my destination from where I am now. If I choose to ignore the guidance of my GPS, I may never reach my destination, but the device will never stop trying to get me back on track.

§

God's Role in Suffering Unrelated to Our Choices

While a GPS device is a fitting metaphor for God's plan in relation to the suffering we bring on ourselves through freedom of choice, it can't throw light on God's role in the tragic events of our lives that have little or nothing to do with our choices. Accidents, calamities, and unexpected illnesses are far more difficult to understand or to reconcile with any plan God allegedly has established for us. When faced with these seemingly random disasters, we Christians often choose to believe that this terrible disruption of our lives is really part of God's plan for us. How else can we explain the inexplicable?

Rabbi Harold Kushner wrote the best-selling book *When Bad Things Happen to Good People* after his son died of progeria, a genetic disease which ages the body so rapidly that a child is old and dying long before his time. The experience drove Kushner to ponder why suffering and death strike the good and innocent, and what role, if any, God plays in our anguish. He realized that this question had deeply troubled the members of his synagogue as they reflected on the suffering of the Holocaust survivors in their midst. Now it was his question too, one that erupted from a broken heart.

I read Kushner's book at the urging of a pastor friend of mine whose son had perished in an automobile accident. He told me the book had done more to help him than anything else had. Kushner's thesis, that what happens to us is not controlled by God except in rare circumstances, struck me forcefully. We live in a world of contingency and apparent randomness, yet unlike the ancients who had only religious explanations for the events of their lives, we now accept natural laws as adequate explanations of most natural occurrences, such as disease, earthquakes, and floods. For instance, if you live in California somewhere near the San Andreas fault at the exact moment that great fissure in the earth's crust must shift to relieve unimaginable pressures building within it, then you will live through the drama and terror of an earthquake, not because God has willed it to happen at that precise moment, but because natural forces intersected with your personal timeline. This is why, Kushner argues, when we suffer we are to comfort each other with the realization that the bad things that happen to us, even though we are good people who do not deserve them, have nothing to do with God's direct will. (Kushner is careful to allow that on rare occasions God can intervene as he wishes.) Still, the Christian affirms that such catastrophes are contrary to God's ultimate will and that they will be abolished in the coming kingdom.

Many Christians object to Kushner's theology. Comforted by the belief that there is a divine reason why bad things happen to believers, and that we must accept our suffering as God's will, they do not recognize the additional anguish this theology imposes on other Christians who find such an explanation not only unsatisfactory, but unbearable. To claim that God is teaching us a truth we need to learn, or making us more dependent on him, or giving us opportunities to grow in grace, or even, at times, punishing us for some misdeed contradicts Jesus' teaching on why people suffer misfortune, as we saw in an earlier section. How is the notion that God corrects us through suffering fundamentally different from the teaching that someone's sin caused his or his family's suffering? Christians quote biblical texts to buttress their conviction that suffering is sent by God to correct our faults, purify our characters, and make us more saintly (see Proverbs 3:11-12, quoted in Hebrews 12:6-11 which we quoted earlier). God is leading us, they say, in every event and in every decision we make. Nothing occurs by chance. As one Christian author recently wrote, "A lamb who found himself in the Valley of the Shadow of Death might conclude that he had been falsely led. It was needful for him to traverse that darkness in order to learn not to fear. The Shepherd is still with him."[8] According to this theology, the events of our lives, even the death of a loved one, are merely threads in the fabric of God's design for us.

A poignant example of how such thinking affects believers who have suffered tragedies unrelated to their personal choices came home to me early in my ministry in Takoma Park, Maryland. A young family with two sons had just moved to Maryland where the father was beginning a career as a government scientist and researcher, and they had joined my congregation. Early one morning, as the mother and her two boys were finishing breakfast, they were startled by a loud crash from the floor above. Racing upstairs, they found their husband and father in the throes of a fatal heart attack. When I spoke with the wife shortly after the funeral, she told me that while she and her sons had been comforted by many of their friends and loved ones, she was devastated by a remark made by a pastor whom she knew and respected. "I am terribly sorry for your loss," he had said, "but now you must discover what God is trying to teach you through this experience."

This shocking comment sparked a horrified response in her mind, which she nevertheless kept to herself: "What are you saying? What could you possibly mean? Am I so dumb that God has to kill my husband to teach me something? What kind of God would do that?"

The pastor was no doubt well-intentioned. He probably meant to convey something like, "As bad as this experience is, there is a purpose behind it, so it isn't a total tragedy." But his belief concerning God's role in the woman's suffering made it worse. For her, to think that she was in any sense responsible for her husband's death was simply unbearable.

William Sloane Coffin, Jr. was the preaching minister of the famed Riverside Church in New York City when he received the tragic news that his son Alex had been killed in an automobile accident. Driving home during a bad storm late at night, Alex had tried to negotiate a "dangerous curve at the edge of South Boston Harbor. He had been in a celebratory mood that night that might have included a beer too many.

His car had crashed through a low seawall into the water around midnight; his passenger escaped, but Alex drowned."[9]

Nationally known as the chaplain of Yale University and one of the first white men to be a Freedom Rider during the Civil Rights movement in the 1960s, Reverend Coffin's grief played out in a very public way. Less than two weeks after his son's funeral, Coffin mounted the pulpit at Riverside Church to preach a sermon about his son's death, an act that surprised his close friends and family. Coffin's biographer writes that this was Coffin's way of navigating through the emotional storm he was experiencing. Distraught, Coffin said that his son, "who had enjoyed beating his old man at every game and in every race, . . . had now beat his father to the grave" (Goldstein, p. 309).

Like the grieving young mother in my own congregation, Coffin had received comments and letters from would-be friends, especially ministers, whose sentiments infuriated him. In his sermon, he singled out one in particular not only for its insensitivity, but for its destructive theology. One of Coffin's old friends implied that Alex's death was God's will.

> This "should never be said," he told the congregation, as he described "swarming all over her," demanding to know if it was "the will of God that Alex never fixed that lousy windshield wiper of his, that he was probably driving too fast in such a storm, that he probably had a couple of 'frosties' too many?" He confessed that "nothing so infuriates me as the incapacity of seemingly

intelligent people to get it through their heads that God doesn't go around this world with his finger on triggers, his fist around knives, his hands on steering wheels." Quite the contrary: "My own consolation lies in knowing that it was not the will of God that Alex die; that when the waves closed over the sinking car, God's heart was the first of all our hearts to break." This argument accounts for why clergy have been using this sermon in grief counseling ever since (Goldstein, p. 310).

Students in my class on Christian Ethics and Healthcare occasionally voice views similar to Coffin's friends. One admirable, courageous woman told me that she believed God had sent her an autistic child because God knew that she could do a good job of handling him because of her expertise in child development. That was the meaning and purpose of her suffering: she was to carry this burden so that someone else would not have to. She believed she had been chosen to bear this cross in God's name. But when I asked her about all the autistic children of parents who had not had child development training, she had no response.

Another student, in answer to an exam question on the ethics of allowing a neonate with severe anomalies to die comfortably, wrote that parents pregnant with a severely retarded child should never consider abortion or even passive euthanasia because it must be God's plan for the couple to raise such a child. Perhaps, she opined, God intends this experience to help the couple grow spiritually. Some students in my class have even wondered whether a hospital's "Do Not Resuscitate" order interferes with God's timetable for a patient's death.

I understand the powerful emotional need to find meaning in an apparently senseless and inexplicable tragedy, personal or collective. My mind too rebels against the meaninglessness of 86,000 deaths after an earthquake in Pakistan, or 250,000 people swept away in an Indian Ocean tsunami. Some believers bring order out of these chaotic events by reasoning that God allowed or even caused such catastrophes for reasons we cannot know. But such thinking misinterprets how God relates to our world and its history. The conviction that everything that happens is within God's plan for each person and for the world as a whole assumes either some form of the old doctrine of predestination, or a Christian form of pagan fatalism that says whatever happens has to be; nothing else could have happened because it would have been outside of God's plan.

§

When Tragedy Strikes, God Has a Plan

I firmly believe that a right understanding of God's relation to us and to history will lead believers to say not, "This tragedy or disappointment is a part of God's plan," but rather, "Now that this tragedy or disappointment has happened, God has a plan." Human freedom means that if I choose to engage in a high-risk activity that leaves me a quadriplegic, my hopes (and God's hopes) for my life will not end, but they will have to be drastically altered. God will work with me and my family to help us rebuild the story of my life. I will become a "wounded storyteller" who must reconstitute my life's narrative. Because this has happened, God will help me develop a plan.

Let me illustrate with a familiar scenario. A young woman is determined to marry a certain young man over the objections of her parents. (My own belief is that if you come from a loving home with wise parents, you would be foolhardy not to take a hard second look at such a decision before you acted on it. But that's another homily.) Fortunately, this young woman has an unusually wise father who decides to take his prospective son-in-law golfing, and as they are walking from the 8th green to the 9th tee, he says, "I know you are well aware of my reservations about this marriage, especially about you being able to keep your marriage commitment as you should. I hope I am wrong, believe me. But I want you to know that now that you and my daughter are going ahead with your plans, I will do everything in my power to support you. And if the marriage falls apart, I will be there to help both of you pick up the pieces."

God is like that father. If we love and trust God, when we stumble and fall, he will help us pick up the pieces of our brokenness. Think again of the actor Michael J. Fox, who did not plan on getting Parkinson's disease, but his misfortune led to another plan: to use his celebrity and influence to help end Parkinson's for those who come after him. He has reshaped the broken pieces of his life into something splendid. In his autobiography he insists that he would not want to go back to the kind of person he was or the life he lived before Parkinson's struck him. The suffering has changed him for the better. Many will be tempted thus to conclude that God sent Fox Parkinson's disease in order to change his life and improve the prospects for a cure. But Fox does not believe that. He believes, as I do, that he was a victim of forces that did not target him personally, but struck him nonetheless. With the help of his wife, family, and friends, he—like another celebrity, Christopher Reeve,—took the materials of a tragedy and reshaped them into a blessing to other people. That is what God helps us do if we love and trust him in our own suffering. When things don't go according to plan, either in our lives or in the events of our world, we must remember that God, the Creator and Redeemer, has promised to help us develop a new plan for our lives, as well as for the world's future, that supports his magnificent, ultimate plan to make all things new. Like a sculptor who takes discarded junk from the town dump, God can take what is and turn it into what ought to be.

I have long loved spirituals, but I have come to admire them even more deeply as I have learned about the profound suffering out of which they came. They gave voice to the faith and hope of people enduring brutality and unspeakable anguish. Without that suffering, I suspect, their music would not have come into being to bless and enrich our lives. Dietrich Bonhoeffer, the famous German theologian martyred during World War II, experienced black worship and music in the Abyssinian Baptist Church in New York City during his year-long study at Union Theological Seminary. He commented later that this was the first time he had heard the gospel preached with real passion and seen Christian believers challenging the State over injustice. The spirituals particularly moved him because they came directly from blacks' experience of oppression. Should we then conclude that God intended slavery in order to ensure the emergence of this powerful form of music? That would be monstrous. On the contrary, God's grace—flowing in the veins of slaves—brought out of their suffering a music that has transformed people in every culture. Because African slaves suffered, God had a plan.

§

Another Way to Understand God and Suffering

In their groundbreaking book *The Openness of God*,[10] Richard Rice and others posit that God does not know the future of each life in every detail because our human freedom cannot be predicted, yet God knows all the possibilities in each life and is prepared for whatever happens. This is quite different from Calvinistic theology, which superimposes God's providence and sovereignty on every event that occurs. Some Christians find the idea that God is open to human events less comforting than "God-in-control" thinking. But whether Rice's theory is true or not, many Christians find it very helpful in the face of tragedy. Those who embrace this position see that there may be countless creative and unpredictable possibilities that determine how their lives intersect with and contribute to God's overall plan for themselves and the world.

Christians who reject the view propounded by Rice and remain convinced that everything that happens is part of a detailed plan formulated by God before they were born seem to find sufficient reason for their suffering in their need for spiritual growth. They seem to believe that their spiritual welfare is of such tremendous importance to God that he will allow them to endure unspeakable suffering if that will ensure their ultimate salvation. God's use of suffering to almost "force" people to be faithful neutralizes the biblical emphasis on God's gift of freedom to us, an essential quality in maintaining the love relationship between human beings and God which makes voluntary (is there any other kind?) faithfulness possible. These well-meaning Christians also fail to make the crucial distinction suggested by the passage in Hebrews 12 quoted earlier in this section: Suffering that results from faithfulness to the Gospel witness ("you will have persecutions") must be viewed differently from the suffering that comes from being a human in an imperfect world, regardless of one's faithfulness. It is obvious that my staying true to Christ in the midst of suffering for the Gospel blesses not only me but all those affected by my experience ("the church has been nurtured by the blood of martyrs"). Suffering that simply happens (my child is born autistic or an accident leaves me a quadriplegic) cannot be attributed to my relationship to God in the same way. Whether a random tragedy results in grace depends on my capacity to cling to God's promises for the future as I endure the ordeal. Believers who trust God in the midst of pointless suffering will indeed find their faith strengthened, but that benefit comes from God's grace, nothing else.

We cannot praise God for the suffering brought on by random, meaningless death and disaster. There simply is no underlying benefit, such as extending the Gospel message, which in itself would make such suffering worth enduring. We must endure it simply to go on with our lives of service to Christ. Paul and Barnabas could sing in prison when they were arrested for preaching, but we cannot sing at the funeral of a child or spouse. God may use that kind of suffering to help us grow in grace only as long as we cling to his promises for the future. If we let him, God will always work with us to bring some good out of suffering, but he does not send it, except in the rarest of circumstances, simply to encourage us to trust him.

It bears repeating that when Christ predicted that his followers would endure trials, he was saying that the political powers of this world will always react violently against the messengers of truth and light in an attempt to discourage them and even destroy their faith. But when God's servants continue to trust him, persecution has the opposite effect, strengthening them for the next battle. When we insist on teaching that God deliberately sends suffering to people—suffering to which only God's grace can impart any meaning—we risk destroying people's faith in a just and compassionate God. Christians who insist on making God directly responsible for every tragic event seldom ponder the nature of a God who would allow someone to endure terrible suffering merely to assist them in their spiritual journey. The Russian novelist Dostoevsky wrote that the suffering and death of children is the single greatest challenge to God's existence and goodness that it is possible to imagine. Yet, for whatever reasons, there are Christians who can only find comfort and security in a God who controls everything that happens.

Clearly, sensitive caregivers should not seek to pull out from under such Christians the rug of divine control on which they stand by simply challenging their viewpoint. One must always listen before speaking and allow people to rely on whatever belief system has sustained them throughout their lives. Yet, should their faith in God's control be shaken by the events in their lives, caregivers may be able to help them by confessing they have found it helpful to think about the issue differently.

§

God's Plan and Our Prayers for Healing

Those who believe that tragedy and sickness are part of God's plan are also inclined to believe that enough prayer and sufficient faith will move God to rescue them from their troubles through miraculous intervention. They reason that if God has the power to send misfortune, he can also intervene to correct the misfortune, especially in the case of life-threatening illness. They believe that their sense of need for God's help will strengthen their faith and make their prayers for a miracle acceptable to God. Their belief in God's miraculous intervention on their behalf may also be based on passages of Scripture such as the following:

> Come now, you who say, "Today or tomorrow we will go into such a town and spend a year there and trade and get gain": whereas you do not know about tomorrow. What is your life? For you are a mist that appears for a little time and then vanishes. Instead you ought to say, "If the Lord wills, we shall live and we shall do this or that." As it is, you boast in your arrogance. All such boasting is evil.
> Is any among you sick? Let him call for the elders of the church, and let them pray over him, anointing him with oil in the name of the Lord; and the prayer of faith will save the sick man, and the Lord will raise him up; and if he has committed sins, he will be forgiven (James 5:13-15).
> As they passed by in the morning, they saw the fig tree withered away to its roots. And Peter remembered and said to him, "Master, look! The fig tree which you have cursed has withered." And Jesus answered them, "Have faith in God. Truly, I say to you, whoever says to this mountain, 'Be taken up and cast into the sea,' and does not doubt in his heart, but believes that what he says will come to pass, it will be done for him. Therefore, I tell you, whatever you ask in prayer, believe that

149

you have received it, and it will be yours" (Mark 11:20-24).

These and other Bible verses have spawned countless faith-healing ministries, from sawdust-strewn tent meetings to slickly produced media extravaganzas. Whether the suffering individuals come up on stage where the minister can press his hand onto their foreheads and shout, "In the name of Jesus, be healed!" or are simply urged to touch their television screens at home, the subsequent "healing" is attributed to the gift of the Holy Spirit. This approach does not require a great deal of faith on the part of those who seek help; the faith is largely provided by the healer, who is the vehicle for God's spirit. Such practices purport to be modeled after the healings Jesus performed on large groups of people, many of whom were not believers.

My personal experience of faith healing came from attending a healing service in Chicago conducted by Kathryn Kuhlman, at that time one of the most prominent healing evangelists in America. I sat near the front of the auditorium to hear and see as much as possible. Kuhlman invited those who wished to be healed to come forward, and several testified that they had been cured of ailments such as neck pain or poor hearing. Just a few feet away from me, a boy in a wheelchair struggled to get to the platform. His father spoke to several of Kuhlman's staff members, asking for help to get the wheelchair up the stairs. They did not respond, and that troubled me greatly for I knew that Jesus cured any and all who came to him. His ministry did not involve selective healing for maximum effect. Overall, the evening with Ms. Kuhlman struck me as a sham.

Not all faith healing is so public or extravagant. Some clergy take a more sophisticated approach to their healing ministry. They claim that if we would receive God's healing, *we* (not they) must exercise the faith that moves mountains. In other words we must believe that our prayer is being answered *even as we are praying*, regardless of whether or not we see any evidence that our prayer is being answered. It is not faith to *hope* God will hear and answer our prayers. Faith requires that we believe God is healing us or the ones for whom we pray *as we pray*.

A leading proponent of this approach is Jim Glennon, whose book *Your Healing is Within You*[11] is being embraced by growing numbers of people. His healing ministry focuses on a deep, disciplined prayer life and the involvement of large numbers of people praying for someone in need. He describes it as a spiritual gift (I Corinthians 12:9, 28), a specific Christian ministry to which all laity are called.

According to this view, receiving a cure requires knowing what God wants of us as Christians and then making sure our prayers are in harmony with God's will. Regarding his promises to cure our diseases, God requires that we believe completely that our prayers are being answered as we utter them, and that we continue believing even if nothing happens. Furthermore, to be effective, the prayer of faith must conform to specific rules. If our faith is equal to the mountain of sickness to be moved, there is no reason why our prayer cannot be answered at once. If our faith is small, and the mountain large, God may give us gradual healing to encourage us to continue to pray and trust, no matter how long it takes (Glennon, pp. 32-33). In other words, for our prayer to be answered, we must believe it is being answered. This is not a contingent promise. According to Glennon, the usual Christian prayer that concludes with "if it be Thy will" is a prayer of doubt that anything will really happen. Instead, he says, we must believe as we pray. God leaves no room for uncertainty or compromise, so any failure to truly believe puts the outcome in doubt.

Nor, says Glennon, is this promise limited to prayers for the sick. Whatever you ask that is consistent with God's will shall be granted. In fact, asking is not even required; it is already present and available. Just accept it. "The kingdom of God is in the midst of you. Your healing is within you" (Glennon, p. 80). To illustrate, Glennon describes the experience of the Baileys of South Australia. Their adopted son Graeme developed a serious back problem that resulted in a hump for which nothing could be done. His heart was being affected, so the parents turned to Scripture, clinging to the belief that God wants to keep his promises of healing. As Glennon put it, the Baileys "were not prepared to take 'no' for an answer" (Glennon, p. 20). They believed God's promise even though nothing happened at first. Then gradually, over a three-year period, as they thanked God in advance for healing Graeme, they saw increasing improvement until Graeme's back was completely straight.

As a contrast, Glennon relates the experience of the McElweys, who did not receive the healing they prayed for because, according to Glennon, their faith must have wavered, so God could not answer their prayer. Glennon warns that when our prayers are not answered, we must accept that this time, for inscrutable reasons, God has decided not to grant his promise.

I find aspects of Glennon's thinking very disturbing. I believe it is God's ultimate will that none of us should ever be sick or die. But to insist that it is God's current plan to cure us of all our afflictions flies in the face of the experience of most believers, as well as the New Testament record. Even the apostle Paul confessed that he had prayed to be relieved of an affliction but that God did not answer his prayer (2 Corinthians 12:8). I have known many believers who prayed for healing with all the faith they could muster, then when they didn't receive the healing they asked for they were told that it was their own fault. Laying on these people the additional burden of failing to manifest sufficient faith is to impose on them, and those who pray for them, a profound guilt. Why does the God who offers us righteousness as a free gift—no works required—not offer us healing as a free gift, no works required? And, if the sick also believe that God caused their illness to teach them something, then they feel doubly responsible for their affliction. To feel responsible for God's failure to answer our prayers is a throwback to the "illnesses" of the New Testament, which we discussed in an earlier section.

Nevertheless, dear friends of mine followed Glennon's program of prayer for their son who contracted the rare and deadly disease known as "aplastic anemia." Almost always fatal, their son—after much prayer—shows no sign of that disease today. He was treated with the standard therapy (which seldom cures), but his parents are convinced that his current "normal" blood reading is an act of God's providence. I do believe God can act as God wishes and would not dispute their belief that God acted on their son's behalf. But, we are still left with the puzzle: why are such acts of God so rare?

§

Does God Answer Some Prayers and Ignore Others?
Two articles published a week apart in The *Adventist Review* (February 14 and 21, 2002) provided the clearest illustration I've seen of the confusion inherent in the issue of prayers for healing. In the first article ("Jessica's Eyes," by Jeannie Buchholz), a young mother told of her joy when her baby's eye condition was healed. She described walking through a shopping mall and being stopped by a concerned woman who noticed the baby's problem. Once the stranger understood the condition and that it would require minor surgery to correct, she asked the mother if she could pray for her child and the mother agreed. The author was deeply touched by the stranger's prayer and wondered why her own church members had

not offered to pray for her and her baby. A short time later, the eye condition healed without surgery.

In an article published a week later ("Where There is Faith," by Sari Fordham), a young graduate student recounted her mother's brave battle with incurable cancer. A devout Christian, the mother was convinced that God would miraculously cure her and resolutely clung to that hope as her church and family members joined her in earnest prayer. The day she died, she cried out to God for relief from her pain, but the ambulance transporting her pain medication got lost on the way to her home and arrived too late. The author describes her own struggle with faith in the following months, and how she maturely and responsibly resolved her theological difficulties. Her struggle with faith touched me, and the contrast between the two articles left me wondering: Why would God honor a stranger's prayer for a minor and treatable ailment and ignore the prayers of family and church members for a cure for a terminal illness? Most Christians invoke God's "mysterious ways" to answer this question, as Glennon does, and even condemn the question itself as borderline blasphemy. But appeals to God's inscrutable ways do not answer heartfelt questions about our relationship to God and his plan for our lives.

A friend of mine told me about two women who worked for a church-operated hospital in Florida who were diagnosed with breast cancer at about the same time. Both were prayed for by the same group of believers in their local church, and both received standard medical treatment for their condition. One died and the other went into apparent remission. In church one morning, the husband of the deceased woman listened as the other woman gave her testimony about what she believed was a cure at God's hands. My friend, who was sitting next to the widower, asked him how it felt to hear this woman describe God's gift of healing—a gift God apparently chose not to give to this man's wife. "Not very good, I can tell you," the man replied.

Tragically, and ironically, the woman who testified in church of her miraculous healing enjoyed only six more months of life before her tumor returned and she died. This episode shocked the hospital community since it seemed that God, instead of answering prayers, had played with people's lives. It is a powerful illustration of what can happen when God's fairness is called into question. The apparently capricious way in which God heals some and not others challenges the theology and faith of those who insist that God's plan is to miraculously cure all believers of their afflictions.

I see several pitfalls in this way of thinking. When we offer prayer for the sick, if we think that God has to provide a cure because we are praying in faith, then we can reassure ourselves that we possess some control over our own destinies. Even though most prayers do not result in cures, many believers are heartened to think that the fault lies with them and not with God. They would rather believe that they have failed than that God has not responded to their pleas. Believers may also fall back on the view that God's plan for each of us is known only to himself. God alone knows whether the cure we prayed for harmonizes with his plan, and therefore, whether or not we are better off with a "no" than with a miraculous healing. Finally, when one Christian is apparently healed through prayer and another is not, it is pernicious mischief to accuse the unanswered believer of insufficient faith.

§

Scientific Studies on the Benefits of Prayer

This is not to say that prayer has no role in ministry to the sick. Christians believe that praying for the sick gives them a sense of God's presence and hope for the future. There is even some scientific research showing that prayer has clear physical benefits. However, research conducted to determine whether or not prayer "works" for the sick has created a significant medical controversy. Initial studies conducted by Dr. Randolph C. Byrd found that cardiac patients who were prayed for had a better outcome.[12] In a clinical trial, patients in a coronary care unit who were prayed for by Christian prayer groups outside the hospital did better than patients who did not receive prayer. The findings were remarkable, given that patients were randomly assigned to the treatment and control groups, neither patients nor hospital staff knew who was in which group, and the patients and those who prayed for them never met. These early findings created enormous excitement among medical and spiritual caregivers who believed deeply that the spiritual dimension is essential to the health of the total person.[13]

However, subsequent studies disputed these findings. Jeremy Manier claims that the largest study ever done on the healing power of prayer showed little impact on patients' health.[14] "Indeed, researchers at the Harvard Medical School and five other U.S. medical centers found, to their bewilderment, that coronary bypass patients who knew strangers were praying for them fared significantly worse than people who got no prayers. The team speculated that telling patients about the prayers may have caused 'performance anxiety,' or perhaps a fear that doctors expected the worst." Ethicist, physician, and Franciscan friar Daniel Sulmasy was quoted as saying: "God is not just another therapeutic nostrum in a doctor's black bag. It seems fundamentally sinful to conceive of God as our instrument." And a Catholic priest conceded that it may be an unfair test of God to measure whether detailed prayers are granted. "The best prayer," he said, "probably is, 'Thy will be done'" (Manier). As we have seen, however, I argue that it is almost never God's direct will that we suffer, only that God's promise to grace us through our illness and suffering is sure.

§

God's Plan—Our Reality

Today, many Christian theologians are uncomfortable with the notion that everything that happens is a preordained part of God's plan for our lives. They believe it minimizes or even negates human freedom and downplays the important role we all have in creating our own identities through our personal choices. No plan has been built into us in advance; no divine script is programming our days. Liberty defines human being. One cannot grow in God's image by playing guessing games about what God has willed for one's life. God's "plan" can be summed up as his overarching desire that each of us make choices in harmony with love and truth, and that we exercise our freedom courageously so that we can enjoy even more freedom.

As with most things concerning the ways of God, this is a profound mystery. But perhaps the picture will become a bit clearer if we can grasp this paradox: God does not plan everything that happens, but nothing that happens is beyond God's power to transform the meaninglessness of our suffering into something redemptive for us and others through divine grace. God knows that natural disasters will claim thousands of lives every year. He knows that sickness and death will touch every human being and every family group, causing unspeakable suffering and sorrow. And, we must never forget, all suffering is felt by God. How then could it be God's intention that these things happen? God does not need to send suffering to teach us a lesson because he knows we are finite and vulnerable, and therefore suffering will find us no matter what we do to avoid it. But when bad things inevitably occur, God has set in motion a plan ensuring that they will not have ultimate significance for our lives or for the world's history. Death and suffering will not be the final chapters in the story of God's universe.

When we face chronic or life-threatening illness, God's plan is to help us grow in grace and faithfulness. If we do not survive, his plan is to restore our lives according to the divine timetable. Our suffering is within God's plan, even if God did not plan our suffering. When the apostle Paul says, "And we know that in all things God works for the good of those who love him, who have been called according to His purpose" (Romans 8:28), he is not saying that everything that happens to us is good because God sent it for our edification. He is saying that because we love God and God loves us, all things—even tragedies—have the potential to weave a web of ultimate meaning and blessing in our lives. God's wisdom, power, and grace will bring out of the mess of this life something transcendent and glorious as ultimate proof that everything is in his hands.

However God created the world in the beginning, it is now a place of contingency—good and bad things can unexpectedly happen that are in themselves devoid of ultimate meaning. When Jesus preached in the Sermon on the Mount (Matthew 5-7) that his followers should love their enemies because God sends the rain on the just and the unjust alike, he meant that God had ordered the world so that, in general, events don't discriminate between the virtuous and the reprobate. When the psalmist challenges Yahweh, "Why do the righteous suffer and the wicked prosper?" the answer is: Because most of the time, that's just the way the world works.

But God's ultimate plan for each individual and for all creation cannot be disrupted by that which intensifies human misery and therefore calls into question God's Lordship over our lives. Not even death can abrogate the biblical truth that eternal life is ours now (John 5:24, 6:27). Regardless of what happens to our body, our future with God is assured.

The English poet Alfred Tennyson, writing in the 19th century, was troubled by the latest geological discoveries and the emerging science of evolutionary biology. He wanted to believe that God knew every sparrow, and that every single thing, no matter how seemingly insignificant, was part of a divine plan. It troubled him to think that things happened randomly or that there was no one with ultimate control over human events. He wanted the universe to be a place of order, truth, and justice. He wrote in his poem "In Memoriam":

> Oh yet we trust that somehow good
> Will be the final goal of ill,
> To pangs of nature, sins of will,
> Defects of doubt, and taints of blood;
>
> That nothing walks with aimless feet;
> That not one life shall be destroy'd,
> Or cast as rubbish to the void,
> When God hath made the pile complete.

In the poem's concluding stanzas, Tennyson reveals his doubts, yet clings to hope:

Behold, we know not anything;
I can but trust that good shall fall

At last—far off—to all,
And every winter change to spring.
So runs my dream: but what am I?
An infant crying in the night:
An infant crying for the light:
And with no language but a cry.

Tennyson's clinging to hope in the face of despair is not unique. In the preface to his remarkable book, *Blindsided*,[15] Richard M. Cohen describes his battle with multiple sclerosis with brutal honesty:

> Within three years, just as my career as a television journalist was ascending in the historic hurricane of Watergate, I was engulfed in my own, very personal storm. Illness came calling when I was twenty-five years of age, and it has never left.

> The once unhampered trek toward a bright horizon has become a shaky walk across moving terrain. The landscape and contours of life have shifted. I have passed from newsrooms through operating rooms to a more reflective existence. The large events of the world, the trembling earth that preoccupies the journalist, have given way to the struggle to sustain a small life.
> My thirty-year effort to salvage that life, to wrest it from the clutches of sickness, has been a search

for control and the perspective to adjust. Survival skills have been honed, forged in one of life's hottest furnaces. What I have learned is that I am stronger and more resilient than ever I imagined. My dysfunctional vision and impaired body are testaments to the damage MS can inflict. Colon cancer has left me with a gut I could not sell at a used car lot, no money down. But as my body weakens, my spirit grows strong and occasionally soars.

Self-pity is poison. There is no time. I need a future and refuse to become a victim. Too often we become oblivious to our own prisons, taking the bars and high walls for granted. Sometimes we construct them ourselves, and the barbed wire goes up even higher. Too many of the limitations placed on us are an extension of our own timidity.[15]

In refusing to escape into victimhood, Cohen is on the side of God. By divine grace, we too can be furious at our fate without giving in to self-pity. We can courageously face uncertainty and suffering, clinging to the hope that is our birthright in this age of medical and technological marvels. We can fight passionately against threats to our lives, bearing in mind that even when the hope of cure is remote, God's healing could not be closer nor his promises more certain.

Notes and References

[1]Kushner, Harold. *When Bad Things Happen to Good People* (New York: Avon Books, 1981).

[2]Hart, David Bentley. *The Doors of the Sea: Where Was God in the Tsunami?* (Grand Rapids, MI: William B. Eerdmans, 2005), 82. I highly recommend this small but insightful volume for a more detailed discussion of this issue.

[3]"Nature's God: Nancey Murphy on Religion and Science" (Interview). *The Christian Century* (December 27, 2005; Vol. 122), pp. 20-26.

[4]Neiman, Susan. *Evil in Modern Thought: An Alternative History of Philosophy* (Princeton, NJ: Princeton University Press, 2004), p. 30.

[5]"Split Over Global Warming Widens Among Evangelicals." *The Wall Street Journal* (September 28, 2007), p. 1.

[6]This assertion needs to be nuanced considerably if it is to make sense in light of the love of God revealed in Christ Jesus. Many millions of Native Americans were wiped out by European diseases and wars in order to clear this land for European settlers. That God had a hand in the events that formed this nation is certainly believable. But from my point of view, God's hand was making the best of a bad situation given the imperialism and arrogance of the European Christian culture of that time.

[7]Sharlet, Jeff. "Through a Glass, Darkly: How the Christian Right is Reimagining U.S. History." *Harper's Magazine* (December 2006), pp. 33-43.

[8]Eliot, Elisabeth. *Quest for Love* (Grand Rapids, MI: Fleming H. Revell, 1996), p. 218.

[9]Goldstein, Warren. *William Sloane Coffin Jr.: A Holy Impatience* (New Haven: Yale University Press, 2004), p. 308.

[10]Pinnock, Clark, Richard Rice, John Sanders, William Hasker, and David Basinger. *The Openness of God: A Biblical Challenge to the Traditional Understanding of God* (Downers Grove, IL: 1994). Richard Rice's original book *The Openness of God* as well as this one have influenced my thinking over the years in many ways.

[11]Glennon, Jim. *Your Healing Is Within You* (Alachua, FL: Bridge-Logos, 1980), pp. 32-33.

[12]Byrd, RC. Positive therapeutic effects of intercessory prayer in a coronary care unit population. *Southern Medical Journal* (1988; Vol. 81), pp. 826-829.

[13]Dossey, Larry. *Healing Beyond the Body: Medicine and the Infinite Reach of the Mind* (Boston: Shambala Pubs., 2001).

[14]Manier, Jeremy. "Study: Prayer Didn't Help Sick." Available at: *http://seattletimes.nwsource.com/cgibin/PrintStory.pl?document_id=2002901053&zsection_id=2002120005&slug=pray31&date=20060331*. Accessed February 2008.

[15]Cohen, Richard M. *Blindsided: A Reluctant Memoir* (New York: HarperCollins, 2004), pp. xv-xvii, passim.

Conclusion

We have seen that in biblical times sickness and physical disabilities were understood very differently than we understand them today. The people of Palestine during the time of Christ had no science that could explain blindness, fever, mental illness, or paralysis. The knowledge and instruments necessary to comprehend the "invisible" organisms and processes responsible for human diseases were more than 1,600 years in the future. As a result, explanations for suffering assumed that God was punishing the sick and disabled for their own sins or the sins of their parents. Being the object of God's disfavor precipitated a crisis for both the sick and the community. After all, how could society support people whom God had clearly rejected? Physical suffering was compounded by the emotional and spiritual burden of being cut off from a public (not to mention some families and friends) which saw them as unclean, polluted, and sinful. That is why Jesus' ministry of healing focused not merely on restoring the body, but also—even primarily—on healing the loneliness and isolation that came from feeling cut off from God and community by sin. When Jesus healed a physical sickness, he also healed the illness of rejection and isolation through forgiveness. Being cured was certainly a cause for rejoicing, but being accepted back into the circle of family and community was the greater gift.

We also saw that Christian spirituality for caregivers might be understood as "feeling the way God feels" about the sick, disabled, and guilt-ridden. While we no longer interpret people's suffering as a direct consequence of their sins, for a variety of reasons we still intentionally or unintentionally cut them off from full participation in the larger social network. To mirror the compassion of Jesus as he lived it during his brief ministry, we must participate wholeheartedly in the suffering of the sick, lonely, and shame-filled.

We then highlighted God's command that we must all rest, especially caregivers whose self-sacrifice for their patients seduces them into compassion burnout. Not resting may turn some of the virtues of physicians, nurses and others into vices. When they take time from caring for their patients in order to care for themselves, when they resist the temptation to work a little harder and to do a little more to ensure superior patient care most caregivers suffer guilt. The sabbath provides balance to this excessively self-denying tendency by reminding us that God's promise to relieve the suffering in this world gives us permission to let go and not make our work for others into an idol. Even Jesus had to retreat and rest from his healing ministry. Why are we tempted to think we do not need such rest?

Lastly, we saw how the belief that the sick are being punished by God for their sins has morphed in the minds of many believers into a conviction that God either intends or permits our suffering for our own or the greater good. And since God has absolute control over human events, anything that happens to us—including sickness and disability—is part of God's plan and we must accept it without complaint. It follows that Christian caregivers who embrace this view believe that the people they are charged to care for are suffering because God has decided they should be. This belief must create a terrible inner tension, for how can you seek to cure people in Christ's name when your theology dictates that God has willed their sickness in the first place?

I believe that this concept of God and his dealings with his Creation is completely wrong-headed and has no place in the Christian ministry of healing. God's purpose has always been, and continues to be, to save us from sin and to heal our afflictions, including the sickness and death imposed on us not by God, but by God's enemy. Death is the ultimate "illness" because it separates us completely from everything life has to offer, especially the people we love and who love us. Christ promised that God is preparing a healing future for us all, one which we will experience in its fullness at his second coming. This hope is planted in the soil of Christ's suffering and resurrection, and grows only by the exercise of faith.

The promise sounds almost too good to be true: No sickness, no loneliness or brokenness brought on by guilt or shame, no separation from other people or from God. The promise of the resurrection of the body at the end of time is a promise of reunion for all the faithful throughout all ages of history (I Thessalonians 4). Free of sickness and death, free from the fear of separation and isolation, we achieve a mutuality and intimacy beyond our wildest dreams.

In his celebrated book *Night*,[1] Elie Wiesel describes watching as several prisoners are hung in the concentration camp. One of them was a small boy who, being so light, writhed on the gallows far longer than the others. Wiesel recalls hearing a voice in the crowd behind him whisper, "Where is God now?" and answering to himself, "Where is God now? He is here, hanging on the gallows." Because the Son of God died on the cross, Christians, too, believe that God is always with the suffering, which makes the questions raised by Christ's delay all the more painful and poignant. Where is God's compassion in the face of human cruelty and indifference? If God truly suffers with his children, why doesn't he end his suffering and ours? If God is God, why doesn't he bring human history to a conclusion and create the Earth anew? Why hasn't the vision of Revelation 22 ("Behold, I make all things new. . . There will be no more crying, neither pain any more, for the former things have passed away") become a reality in our time?

There may be no answers to these questions. Yet we have seen that answers which put God in control of each event in our lives—including our tragedies—are bankrupt because (a) it means we cannot cause our own difficulties with poor choices or (b) that God does not allow natural events in the world to proceed (for the most part) without divine regulation. It also means that efforts to explain all human suffering (not just suffering for the sake of the gospel) as a tool in God's hands to spiritually strengthen or educate us are weak because they proffer a picture of God that contradicts the New Testament teaching that God is love and that we are not "punished" for our sins or weaknesses. In the end, answers to these questions are obscured in the fog of human experience. But believers ultimately believe that God's triumph over death and suffering is guaranteed for us all, and that we and the world we live in will one day be forever healed. The future gives us hope for complete renewal and the present offers us the hope of God's peace, comfort and strength as we anticipate that future.

For believers, that is enough.

Notes and References

[1] Wiesel, Elie. *Night* (New York: Hill & Wang, 1960).